Replenishment Triggers: Setting Systems for Make to Stock, Make to Order & Assemble to Order

**Shaun
Snapp**

For information about this title or to order other books and/or electronic media, contact the publisher:

SCM Focus Press
PO Box 29502 #9059
Las Vegas, NV 89126-9502
http://www.scmfocus.com/scmfocuspress
(408) 657-0249

ISBN: 978-1-939731-55-5

Printed in the United States of America

Contents

CHAPTER 1

Introduction

The terms **make to order** and **make to stock** roll easily off of people's tongues regardless of their knowledge of other supply chain terms. Many executives speak about "moving to a make to order environment." These terms are specific types of manufacturing environments. They are embedded in almost all supply planning applications ranging from the most basic ERP to the most sophisticated advanced planning system. However, if you question supply managers further, you will soon find that many cannot name and are often unfamiliar with the other types of manufacturing environments. In fact, often, what is thought to be one type of manufacturing environment is actually something else entirely. When a businessperson uses these terms, they are thinking of how they will decide when to begin production or procurement for an item. When a systems specialist is thinking of these terms, they are normally thinking about how to select the requirements strategy in order to match the business model. How the forecast is applied is referred to as the requirements strategy in most supply planning systems, be it an ERP system or an external supply planning system. Essentially, requirements strategies control what drives the replenishment of supply. In most cases, the requirement strategies control whether the forecast or the sales order triggers replenishment. However, a related control is over how the forecast is consumed. And in some systems, the requirements strategy also controls whether an availability check is performed.

Requirements strategies are one of the more confusing areas of supply planning. Many consultants have a hard time explaining how requirements strategies work. If this book has no other benefit, it will at least cut down the amount of time that is required for people in companies to understand the relationship between manufacturing environments (the business) and requirements strategies (the technology setting in the supply planning application). This book is designed to bridge the gap between the business side and the systems side of supply management. Business people and IT specialists should be able to read it and understand all of the alternatives with respect to manufacturing environments and their associated requirements strategies.

The Confusing Nature of Requirements Strategies

When one speaks of a requirements strategy it is easy to lapse into the oversimplified view that a bill of materials (BOM) has a single requirements strategy, when in fact, a BOM really has a combination of requirements strategies. By combining various requirements strategies in a single BOM, the supply planning application can be made to meet the requirements of various manufacturing environments. In fact, the overall product location database can be thought of as a matrix, which is connected through a series of BOMs and each material in any given BOM has some requirements strategy assignment that tells the material how to behave. In this book we will explain very specifically how each material in the BOM has a particular requirement strategy and what this means for the replenishment of the item.

Books and Other Publications on Manufacturing Environments

As with all my books, I performed a comprehensive literature review before I began writing. One of my favorite quotations about research is from the highly respected RAND Corporation, a "think tank" based in Santa Monica, CA. RAND's *Standards for High Quality Research and Analysis* publication makes the following statement about how its research references other work.

> *"A high-quality study cannot be done in intellectual isolation: It necessarily builds on and contributes to a body of research and analysis. The relationships between a given study and its predecessors should be rich and explicit. The study team's understanding of past research should be evident in many aspects of its work, from the way in which the problem is formulated and approached to the discussion of the findings and their implications. The team should take particular care to explain the ways in which its study agrees, disagrees, or otherwise differs importantly from previous studies. Failure to demonstrate an understanding of previous research lowers the perceived quality of a study, despite any other good characteristics it may possess."*

This is the first book to focus entirely on manufacturing environments and requirement strategies. It is of course not the first coverage of either topic, as requirements strategies are covered in enterprise software books while manufacturing environments are covered in business books. However, considering how commonly these terms are used on projects and in executive suites, I was surprised that I was only able to find four books with the terms **make to stock**, **make to order**, **assemble to order** or **engineer to order**. These books are: *Product Customization* by Lars Hvam and Niels Henrik Mortensen, *Make-to-Order Lean: Excelling in a High-Mix, Low Volume Environment* by Greg Lane, *Build to Order and Mass Customization* by David M. Anderson, and *Custom Nation: Why Customization Is the Future of Business and How to Profit From It* by Anthony Flynn and Emily Flynn Vencat. Interestingly, all of these books are focused on promoting something called mass customization. They centered on proposing this concept that a key business strategy to adopt is providing more customization, and they tend to focus on companies that have been successful at providing customization. This book takes a different approach. This book is about presenting the options; it does not take a position that a company should be using a particular requirements strategy. My experience, in consulting with a variety of companies, is that there is a very serious need for a book that explains how manufacturing environments and specific requirements strategies connect. I would argue that, before any one particular strategy is followed, it is actually most important to understand the manufacturing environments in detail and how this connects to the requirements strategies. This is because, no matter what requirements strategy is followed, it must eventually be implemented and made to work in a software application.

The Use of Screen Shots in the Book

I consult in some popular and well-known applications, and I've found that companies have often been given the wrong impression of an application's capabilities. As part of my consulting work, I am required to present the results of testing various applications. The research may show that a well-known application is not able to perform some functionality well enough to be used by a company, and point to a lesser-known application where this functionality is easily performed. Because I am routinely in this situation, I am asked to provide evidence of the testing results within applications, and screen shots provide this necessary evidence.

Furthermore, some time ago, it became a habit for me to include extensive screen shots in most of my project documentation. A screen shot does not, of course, guarantee that a particular functionality works, but it is the best that can be done in a document format. Everything in this book exists in one application or another, and nothing described in this book is hypothetical.

Timing Field Definitions Identification

This book is filled with lists. Some of these lists are field definitions. The way to quickly identify which lists are field definitions, they will be all *italics*, while lists that are not field definitions will be only *italics* for the term defined, while the definition that follows is in normal text.

How Writing Bias Is Controlled at SCM Focus and SCM Focus Press

Bias is a serious problem in the enterprise software field. Large vendors receive uncritical coverage of their products, and large consulting companies recommend the large vendors that have the resources to hire and pay consultants rather than the vendors with the best software for the client's needs.

At SCM Focus, we have yet to financially benefit from a company's decision to buy an application showcased in print, either in a book or on the SCM Focus website. This may change in the future as SCM Focus grows – but we have been writing with a strong viewpoint for years without coming into any conflicts of interest. SCM Focus has the most stringent rules related to controlling bias and restricting commercial influence of any information provider. These "writing rules" are provided in the link below:

http://www.scmfocus.com/writing-rules/

If other information providers followed these rules, we would be able to learn about software without being required to perform our own research and testing for every topic.

Information about enterprise supply chain planning software can be found on the Internet, but this information is primarily promotional or written at such a high level that none of the important details or limitations of the application are exposed; this is true of books as well. When only one enterprise software application is covered in a book, one will find that the application works perfectly; the application operates as expected and there are no problems during the implementation to bring the application live. This is all quite amazing and quite different from my experience of implementing enterprise software. However, it is very difficult to make a living by providing objective information about enterprise supply chain software, especially as it means being critical at some point. I once remarked to a friend that SCM Focus had very little competition in providing untarnished information on this software category, and he said, "Of course, there is no money in it."

The Approach to the Book

By writing this book, I wanted to help people get exactly the information they need without having to read a lengthy volume. The approach to the book is essentially the same as to my previous books, and in writing this book I followed the same principles.

1. **Be direct and concise.** There is very little theory in this book and the math that I cover is simple. While the mathematics behind the optimization methods for supply and production planning is involved, there are plenty of books, which cover this topic. This book is focused on software and for most users and implementers of the software the most important thing to understand is conceptually what the software is doing.

2. **Based on project experience.** Nothing in the book is hypothetical; I have worked with it or tested it on an actual project. My project experience has led to my understanding a number of things that are not covered in typical supply planning books. In this book, I pass on this understanding to you.

3. **Saturate the book with graphics.** Roughly two-thirds of a human's sensory input is visual,and books that do not use graphics—especially educational and training books such as this one—can fall short of their purpose. Graphics have also been used consistently and extensively on the SCM Focus website.

Important Terminology

This book will use a variety of terminology that it is necessary to know in order to understand the book. These terms are divided into different categories.

The SCM Focus Site

As I am also the author of the SCM Focus site, http://www.scmfocus.com, the site and the book share a number of concepts and graphics. Furthermore, this book contains many links to articles on the site, which provide more detail on specific subjects. This book provides an explanation of how supply and production planning software works and aims to continue to be a reference after its initial reading. However,if your interest in supply planning software continues to grow, the SCM Focus site is a good resource to which articles are continually added.

The SCM site dedicated specifically to demand planning is http://www.scmfocus.com/supplyplanning

Intended Audience

This book is for anyone interested in better understanding safety stock and service level and, particularly, how to improve how they are set. However, the book also should be of interest to anyone that works in supply chain management systems – both ERP and external planning systems. A final group that could benefit from the book would be those that manage supply chain departments. If you have any questions or comments on the book, please e-mail me at shaunsnapp@scmfocus.com.

Related Books

For those that are interested in the other major control in supply planning, which is the procedure, I recommend the SCM Focus Press book Supply Planning in MRP, DRP and APS Software.[1]

Abbreviations

A listing of all abbreviations used throughout the book is provided at the end of the book.

Corrections

Corrections and updates, as well as reader comments, can be viewed in the comment section of this book's web page. If you have comments or questions, please add them to the following link:

http://www.scmfocus.com/scmfocuspress/supply-books/requirements-strategies/

---

[1] http://www.scmfocus.com/scmfocuspress/supply-books/the-supply-planning-with-mrp-drp-and-aps-software-book/

CHAPTER 2

The Different Manufacturing Environments

Something to first establish is that the term manufacturing environment is probably not the best term that could have been developed to describe this topic, because most companies require a mixture of these environments, even within one factory. The term environment is a very global term and sounds a bit like something related to the factory itself. Perhaps "manufacturing strategy" would have been better – however manufacturing strategy is a highly generalized term that has no specific meaning. While manufacturing environment has a very specific meaning – in a nutshell, it is when production and procurement commences in relation to a demand signal.

There are many manufacturing environments. Each mean specific things in terms of the published literature on the topic and within enterprise software applications. In industry, it is normally not known that **make to stock** is a specific manufacturing environment; therefore lets discuss the different environments and their applications.

The Major Manufacturing Environments

The following are the major manufacturing environments.

1. *Make-to-Stock (MTS, a.k.a. Build-to-Stock or Build-to-Forecast):* Here the replenishment is triggered on the basis of a forecast. Probably mis-named, MTS should actually probably have been called make to forecast, as the forecast is the **trigger** for replenishment – which of course results in stock until the actual sales order arrives.

2. *"Engineered to Order (ETO):* An engineer-to-order approach is one in which a company designs and manufacturers a product based on very specific customer requirements. Because the end product tends to be complex, customers engage with the ETO company throughout the entire design and manufacturing phases to ensure their specifications are met.

3. *Make-to-Order (MTO, a.k.a. Build-to-Order):* This approach is also referred to as build-to-order (BTO) and focuses primarily on production strategy. Some of the required components are stocked whereas more expensive or highly customized parts may need to be produced. Production only starts after an order is received.

4. *Assemble-to-Order (ATO):* Using this environment, companies will have some sub-assemblies already built, stocked and ready to assemble based on the customers' requirements. Once an order is received, final assembly begins and the product is delivered with the appropriate specifications. A key advantage to an ATO environment is minimal inventory is required and the final product can be delivered quickly.

An important feature of the various manufacturing environments is that the **relationship** between the demand signal and the beginning of production or procurement is not always the same for all of the products in the BOM or recipe. For instance, in MTS, all procurement and production is performed **before** the sales order is received. In both ETO and MTO all of the procurement and production is performed **after** a sales order is received – with the products in the BOM for Engineering-to-Order being procured and produced the latest as, at the time of the receipt of the sales order, it is not known exactly what is to be built. However, with Assemble-to-Order, procurement is performed before the sales order is received; however production is performed after the sales order is received. At the heart of the question of which manufacturing environment to use, is the tradeoff between not producing items that will not be in demand versus the efficiency of producing items in large quantities.

All of that seems simple enough, but something that should be remembered, but is often forgotten, is that the manufacturing environments that are available to a company have less to do with what the company "wants to do," and more to do with the particular product the companies produces combined with the type of market that the product is sold to. In markets or submarkets where customization is more important than volume or cost to the consumer, production can be postponed until **after** the sales order. In markets or submarkets where costs are more important and there are little in the way of benefits of customization for the product (light bulbs for instance) production should be performed prior to the receipt of the sales order. It should also be observed that multiple manufacturing environments are employed for the same category of product. For instance, one can either buy a dress shirt from Brooks Brothers in a store, which was produced with a make to stock manufacturing environment, or can provide one's measurements to a tailor and have the shirt custom made in a make to order manufacturing environment.

The Unique Manufacturing Environment of Engineered to Order

It is confusing as to what exactly engineering to order is with respect to supply planning. If "what is to be produced" is not yet agreed upon, it would seem strange that a sales order would be created at all. There is a type of transaction in ERP systems, as well as CRM systems called a quotation. The quotation **precedes** the sales order. A quotation is essentially a request for information – which is normally a price, but can be other information as well. If a sales order has to go through a significant amount of coordination and estimation work, a supply chain system does not actually need to see the sales order. It can rely upon the forecast. The quotation would be the right transaction to use when there is a **higher probability** that the inquiry will actually lead to a sales order. Quotations generally do not flow through to supply planning, as they are not committed demand.

The degree of interaction between companies with respect to engineering to order is explained in the following quotation from the bill of materials software vendor Arena Solutions.

> *"Typically with the engineered-to-order approach, production information and specifications are constantly moving between the ETO company and the customer. Because most product data (design specifications, requirement files, engineering changes, etc.) is often tossed back and forth several times between the ETO company and the customer, either party can become confused if the exchange of product information is poorly managed. For example, it might be difficult to answer questions like how much and what inventory should be lined up for production. Because engineered-to-order products are well-tailored, they are often built from difficult to source parts, expensive parts and highly engineered components. Acquiring the necessary product components can be both a time consuming and costly endeavor causing issues before and during production runs."*
>
> – Engineering to Order

However, in some industries, particularly in products with electrical components, it turns out to be quite common for the companies to submit sales orders to their suppliers that must be engineered/configured before production can begin. In these situations, a high percentage of these orders do eventually become built. In the case where the sales order has a high likelihood of coming to fruition, it does make sense to enter the demand as a sales order. However, a primary benefit of this is that it would allow the supplier to procure the material in the BOM prior to the production date, providing a faster order cycle time to the customer. In this way, engineering to order can simply be considered as make to order but with a much greater delay in production and procurement after the sales order is created.

Engineered to order is a perplexing manufacturing environment for supply chain management for the following reasons:

1. *Changing the Rules of the Transaction Location:* In all other manufacturing environments, the sequence is for the BOM or recipe to be created

by engineering and when complete to be transferred to the ERP system. Up until this time, the supply chain systems **do not even see** the BOM or recipe. This is a good thing because, during product development, the BOM or recipe are going through constant revision. Supply chain systems have enough problems with managing BOMs and recipes without having to deal with a number of intermediate BOMs and recipes that will never be sold.[1] Engineering to order switches the normal sequence by adding the sales order into the supply chain system before the BOM or recipe is complete. In order for the supply chain system to make sense of the sales order, it is necessary to assign a sales BOM or sales recipe to the sales order. This is a proxy for the real BOM because the final BOM is not known at the time that the sales order is accepted. Once the final BOM is determined, a new sales order can be created and the old sales order deleted. This new sales order is assigned to the final BOM version, and this can be done when the final configured product is actually ready to be scheduled for procurement and production.

2. *The Missing Replenishment Trigger:* Engineered to Order it is the only manufacturing environment where **neither the forecast nor the sales order** initiates production or procurement. Rather, there is a further confirmation step, often quite a bit after the sales order is accepted, that finally initiates production and procurement. Supply planning systems (both ERP and external specialized systems) typically use demand (sales orders or forecasts)or the consumption based approach – such as when the planned or actual inventory level drops below a reorder point in order to initiate production and procurement. For this reason, the trigger is typically performed manually. This is explained in Chapter 4: Requirement Strategies.

---

[1] Optimally the interaction on the BOM or recipe will be managed through a dedicated BOM or recipe management systems – often referred to as a PLM or product life cycle system. In fact, unknown to many people with a supply chain rather than product management background, the ERP system should never be the system of record for the BOM or recipe. This is a very interesting and often misunderstood topic that is covered in great detail in the SCM Focus Press Book *The Bill of Materials in Excel, ERP, Planning and PLM/BMMS Software.*

Certainly the most well-known manufacturing environments are MTO and MTS. However, it's important to understand all of the manufacturing environments in order to understand what is available. Companies tend to not have a great deal of control over their manufacturing environment as it tends to be dictated by the relationship between the company and their customers. In different markets, and different categories of that market, there are different customer expectations regarding how much customers are willing to accept between when the order is placed and when the item is received.

Conclusion

An important feature of the various manufacturing environments is that the relationship between the **demand signal** and the **beginning of production or procurement** is not always the same for all of the products in the BOM or recipe. In MTS environments, all procurement and production is performed before the sales order is received. In both Engineering-to-Order and Make-to-Order all of the procurement and production is performed after a sales order is received – with the products in the BOM for Engineering-to-Order being the procured and produced the latest after the sales order is received as at the time of the receipt of the sales order, it is not known exactly what is to be built.

While it is sometimes presented as if the manufacturer can simply choose the manufacturing environment they want to use, in reality, the manufacturing environments that are available to a company have less to do with what the company "wants to do," and more to do with the particular product the companies produces combined with the type of market that the product is sold to.

CHAPTER 3

Triggering Replenishment

This chapter is actually a primer for the next chapter. I believe this is the right sequence because so much of Chapter 4: Requirements Strategies depends upon understanding replenishment triggers. I could have limited the coverage of replenishment triggers narrowly, but upon reflection, I don't think that is the best way to transfer the knowledge around this topic. Therefore, I will cover replenishment triggers broadly in this chapter, including planning triggers and execution triggers. Once this topic is fully understood, requirements strategies come into better focus.

Replenishment Triggers

Replenishment triggers are actions that cause replenishment to occur. The term replenishment is easy to comingle in one's mind with purchasing. However, the replenishment strategy drives both procured materials and produced materials. To replenish simply means **to fill again**. But when we speak about replenishment, we're not just discussing the inventory to be sold, we're also talking about the raw materials needed to produce the inventory and support it's manufacturing. To understand this complex system of supplies that will need replenishing, let's talk about supply networks.

A **supply network** is an association of locations – factories, distribution centers, retail locations and the like. The network will have a series of stocking locations. Supply planning is the determination of the timing and quantity of replenishment across this supply network.

The analysis work that planners stems from this question: when will each stocking location run out of any given material good? Supply planning systems only need to replenish the stocking location when there is good reason to do so, as the objective of supply planning is to **minimize inventory** and **maximize service level**. Across a supply network there are both planning and execution triggers. Some of these triggers are system determined – either ERP, external supply planning system, or warehouse management. Some triggers are external to the system. No matter whether the trigger is system generated or generated by a buyer or IT specialist, all replenishments are,at some point, reflected in the supply planning system with both a transaction (acquisition or goods or sale or product)and a change to the stock holding position at the stocking location. To be clear, let us declare the types of triggers available to the supply network:

Supply Planning System Generated Triggers

These triggers are created through planning runs – or automated procedures that take demand or consumption and create automated replenishment recommendations. The demand oriented supply planning system replenishment triggers are forecasts and sales orders – or projected demand and confirmed demand. The consumption oriented replenishment triggers are based upon the monitoring of stocking locations – and triggered when the stocking location falls below a preset level. This level is called the **reorder point**.[1]In reorder

---

[1] After analyzing reorder point planning for some time I have concluded that reorder points are greatly misunderstood, and in fact unfairly maligned. Reorder points are generally considered to be an outdated approach, however reorder points are simply one supply planning method that is available to be leveraged, and works well in a specific scenario. Reorder points are most useful when future demand crosses a certain threshold of forecast inaccuracy. There is also the misimpression that reorder points have to be very simple, or that they are overly simple. How the reorder point is set can actually be quite sophisticated. However, many vendors tend to offer simple methods of performing reorder point planning in their applications. For instance reorder points in SAP APO

point planning, orders are not triggered by a specific requirement (such as a forecast or dependent requirement), but by hitting a minimum stock level or reorder point. Production orders, purchase orders, and stock transfer orders are simply generated based upon the **relationship** between the stocking level and the reorder point. Any product that receives a level forecast assignment using a best-fit procedure will essentially have their supply planning emulated by using a reorder point. Therefore, the following are the standard replenishment triggers for supply planning for what I call the initial supply planning run – sometimes referred to as the MRP run. This run creates planned production orders and purchase requisitions:

1. *Forecasts:* This is unconfirmed demand. It is what the company thinks it will sell.

2. *Sales Orders:* This is confirmed demand.

3. *Reorder Point:* This is a trigger based upon the stock level. If the stock level or the projected stock level (some supply planning systems will trigger a replenishment based upon a projected stock level rather than the current stock level) is below the order point, then a new replenishment order is created.

In addition to the initial, or MRP, planning run, it is necessary to move material through the supply network and out to the final consumer. This is referred to as the deployment or sometimes the DRP (Distribution Requirements Planning) run. I will not spend much time covering DRP. DRP is covered in detail in the SCM Focus Press book *Supply Planning with MRP, DRP and APS Software*. Deployment replenishment triggers can typically be setup as either push or pull.

---

versus SAP ERP are both relatively simple (although there are quite a few alternatives in terms of how reorder points are set), and also described in this blog article for SAP ERP. MCA Solutions (now Servigistics) has an innovative and relatively sophisticated approach to reorder points by allowing a reorder point to be applied for multiple items. The reorder point is equal to the reorder quantity minus the inventory position. It includes the following values as inputs to the reorder quantity calculation: (where are the values?)

1. *Push:* This means that the sending location creates stock to transport before the demand signal arrives at the receiving location.

2. *Pull:* In a pull configuration, the sending location waits until a demand signal appears at the receiving location.

Fixed Order Cost for a Part

The Network Forecast at the Root Location multiplied by the Condemnation Rate (the average annual percentage at which the product is scrapped) at the Root Location

1. Period in Years

2. Annual Holding Cost

In this way, push or pull deployment is **very similar** to the requirements strategy, which is used for the initial or MRP supply planning run and which will be covered in the next chapter.

Execution Triggers

Supply chain management can be segmented into **planning** and **execution** areas. Planning looks into the more distant future and attempts to make decisions that put the supply chain in the best possible position to meet demand given certain restrictions. Execution is the actual doing, the execution of the plan. For instance, creation of a purchase requisition does not cause anything to actually happen, because a purchase requisition is a planning transaction, not an execution transaction. However, once a purchase requisition is converted into a purchase order – now the order is sent to a supplier and, at that point, the "wheels" begin turning. Accounting entries are posted and physical things begin to happen within the supply chain.

Execution triggers exist in both ERP systems and warehouse management or WM systems. One example of an execution replenishment trigger that will be explained in order to illustrate the differences between a planning trigger and an execution trigger is the KANBAN functionality within some ERP systems. To illustrate this type of trigger, I will be using the KANBAN functionality within the SAP ERP system.

KANBAN

A KANBAN signal is a 100% pull approach. Imagine a machine processing a material, the creation of a KANBAN system means that the work center has no preproduction material to process. Without an immediate transfer of material to its staging area it will have to cease operations. KANBAN is the movement of material triggered by the act of emptying a bin of material. KANBAN is not an inventory management technique, but an inventory release scheduling technique. It is an immediate need signal or trigger. This is described in the graphic below:

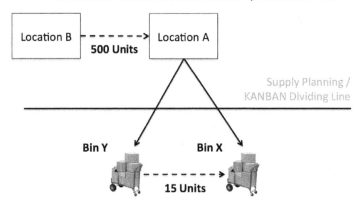

KANBAN Versus Supply Planning

Supply Planning Controlled
- Controls Location to Location Movements
- Locates 500 Units at Location A based upon Reorder Point

KANBAN Controlled
- Controls Interior Location Movements
- KANBAN schedules 15 units to be moved between bins when bin X is empty

The bins shown above are modeled as storage locations in SAP ERP. Storage locations are used to model inventory holding positions within on location. Materials are tracked through the storage locations with goods issues and goods receipts.

Using KANBAN Along with MRP?

SAP ERP actually allows MRP[2] to be run with KANBAN. For a planning professional, this is confusing. It is also interesting, as this functionality is not provided with any of the supply planning or production planning methods in SAP APO. Here is the quote from the SAP documentation.

> *"The materials are planned in the planning run and corresponding procurement proposals are created. These procurement proposals do not directly trigger replenishment but provide a preview of future consumption. In this process, replenishment is also triggered by the Kanban signal."*
>
> – SAP KANBAN Document / PPKAB

This allows the KANBAN system to actually create the procurement proposals.[3] KANBANs have no lead-time – they are signals for immediate replenishment; therefore, they are not useful in creating a material movement signal unless the material is available in the same location, or in a location that is extremely nearby to the facility.[4] Thus, if KANBAN is run along with MRP, it is still necessary to use reorder points to plan the stock and the supplying location for the KANBAN storage location.

For instance, a KANBAN can be setup to point to three different sources of supply:

1. Using in-house production.

2. Using an external source. (or procurement from another plant)

3. Using a stock transfer from another storage location.

---

[2] MRP or Material Requirements Planning, and is one of the five major methods of performing supply and production planning. I have a calculator which shows how MRP works available at this link http://www.scmfocus.com/supplyplanning/2014/04/10/mrp-requirements-calculator/. A fully history of MRP is available at this link http://www.scmfocus.com/scmhistory/2012/08/the-history-of-mrp-and-drp/.

[3] However, while this is possible I cannot think of a reason why I would want to configure a system this way.

[4] This was incidentally was the original design and concept behind supermarkets as run by Toyota – the external facilities were supplier managed mini-warehouses.

When working with an external source, the supply must have stock when the KANBAN signal is received and therefore must be planned. Therefore, the MRP run, which is combined with KANBAN, must be thought of as a separate planning run. It has a different scope and would be on a different planning cycle. For instance, it is quite likely that the plant planners would want to run MRP interactively throughout the day to trigger the KANBAN orders when they have time to deal with them. This is described in the graphic below. It is beneficial to compare this image to the graphic that preceded it. Under this design, notice how the supply planning versus KANBAN dividing line has moved upwards giving the KANBAN / MRP combination a larger scope.

KANBAN with MRP

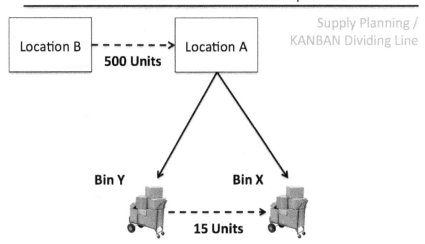

Supply Planning Controlled
- Controls *Stocking at Location B*
- Locates 500 Units at *Location B* based upon Reorder Point

KANBAN with MRP Controlled
- Controls *no Lead Time Location to Location* Movements and Interior Location Movements
- KANBAN schedules 15 units to be moved between bins when bin X is empty, and no lead time movements into Location A with the help of a special KANBAN MRP run.

In conventional MRP procedures, production quantities and dates are calculated in accordance with actual customer requirements and the required quantity and dates of the components are calculated by exploding the bill of material. Exploding the bill of material is performed by MRP and any other supply planning method, takes the quantity of the finished good that is demanded and then multiplies this by the components and subcomponents that are required to support the production of the finished good.

The production quantities can be compiled for various requirements. The creation of **lot sizes** (discrete quantities of a good to be produced at a given time) is based on the selected lot sizing procedure. The exact sizes matter because, in each production level, the lots are usually produced completely before being passed on for further processing. The dates calculated in MRP are the results of a detailed planning run for the current production level even if it is not known exactly when the material is required for the subsequent production level at the time of the planning run. The material is pushed through production on the basis of these dates. This often leads to queue times before production can be started or until the material can be processed further. These queue times are planned as increased lead-times and are rarely undercut. This results in high inventory and longer lead-times in production. KANBAN can be run as a trigger or not run as a trigger depending upon the configuration. This is explained in the following quotation.

> *"The materials are planned in the planning run and corresponding procurement proposals are created. These procurement proposals do not directly trigger replenishment but provide a preview of future consumption. In this process, replenishment is also triggered by the kanban signal."*
>
> – SAP KANBAN Document / PPKAB

Therefore, while SAP says there are two options, KANBAN with MRP and KANBAN without MRP (or normal KANBAN), it should be understood that KANBAN with MRP is just for visibility and does not trigger orders.

Supply Planning Versus KANBAN

Supply planning operates at the level above KANBAN. If the supply plan has not been effective, then there is literally no material to "KANBAN." As execution replenishment triggers deal with moving material already in the supply network, **rather than bringing material into the supply network,** I am not including them in the discussion. When a pure supply planning system is used – such as an APS system, these types of "lower level" triggers are typically not available within the applications.

Physical or Manual Triggers

The flow of orders between facilities is designed in supply planning systems to model hard starts and stops that are part of a sequential flow where one process is finished before another one starts. For instance, the following steps are often followed in this sequence:

1. A production order is initiated in a plant, which produces a finished good based upon a sales order.

2. The plant then places a request on a subcomponent plant (let's say the subcomponent plant is internal to the same company).

3. The subcomponent plant is then planned by the supply planning system to produce the entire quantity of the requirement, which is then shipped in a complete fashion consistent with the transportation, goods issue and goods receipt lead-times that are setup in the system.

4. The finished goods facility then begins processing through all of the subcomponents that are in the factory in the full production need quantities until it has completed the number of units that make up the finished goods production orders.

However, this standard model is not how all factories or locations in a company's supply chain operate. That chain of events does not include the discussion of forces outside of the system, or even manual or equipment driven activities that can trigger replenishment. Instead of waiting until all of the subcomponents are produced at the subcomponent factory to ship them, some companies ship their work product incrementally to other facilities further up the supply chain as production continues. This creates a "continuous flow" between the factories. The individual shipments are incremental shipments that are connected to the requirements for a single production order. This is explained by the graphic below:

Supply Planning for Integrated Factories?

Production Order
For Product A for 5000 Units
Beginning Jan 1st to Jan 10th

Subcomponent STR/STO
For Product A, Daily Shipment of
500 Units Beginning
Jan 1st, continuing every day until
Jan 10th

Q: Can this be controlled by reorder point at location B?
A: *Probably not because the truck is on a milk run between the two locations, and will ship whatever is available at when the truck arrives*

Planned by the Truck's Arrival or by an Incremental Stock Transport Order?

There is a need for continuous flow between finished goods manufacturing facilities and sub-component manufacturing facilities. There are several ways for accounting for this in the system. How it is accounted for depends upon how the company wants to manage the movement of materials between the locations. There are two basic options:

1. Allow the truck's arrival to control the movement timing and quantity between the systems.

2. Allow the supply planning system to control the movement between the facilities.

These options are shown in the two graphics below:

Option 1: The Truck's Arrival is the Move Signal (both in time and quantity)

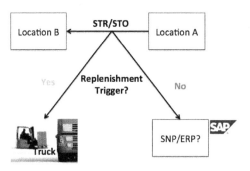

Option 2 is shown below:

Option 2: Supply Planning System Triggers the Movement

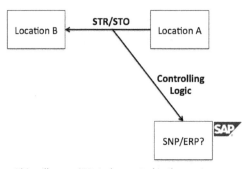

- This will cause STRs to be created in the maximum order quantity entered into the product location master / in this case 500. But it will create 500 unit STRs roughly daily.
- The reorder point could be set at whatever level is desired.

The decision depends upon how the company wants to manage the flow of material between the plants. If the truck leaves with whatever is currently ready for shipment at the time, then truck is actually producing the move signal.

This is the design of many "milk runs" in which a truck simply drives in pre-defined route every day, or every few days. Often, the desire is to maintain a consistent schedule, which means that the truck does not wait for a certain amount of production to be completed, but rather picks up whatever is available. The advantage of this approach is that while the quantity the plants will receive is not known, the time of arrival essentially is. Under this design, the stock transport order is created just a few minutes before the goods issue and an inventory count is performed at the source plant's shipping dock. In this case, the external supply planning system is not involved in decision-making, and the ERP system is simply used to record what occurred.

A second approach is to have the truck wait until production to the planned stock transport order is complete. In this case the stock transport requisition is planned in the external supply planning system, say for example APO / SNP, and then converted to a stock transport order (STO). The shipping department is then responsible for meeting this quantity. In order to ship a quantity, which matches this STO with a **continuously running production line,** it can become necessary to postpone the truck's departure. This means that while the quantity to be shipped and received is more or less guaranteed, **the time the truck arrives at the receiving location is unknown and based upon manufacturing variances**. It also means that the truck will have a lower capacity as its operational window. The time it is actively loading, unloading and transporting freight has effectively been reduced.

Supply planning software is normally designed and setup to manage factories as if they are not part of an integrated production line. Some finished goods are made composed of multiple production lines that are distributed among various facilities as part of a "superplant."This is covered in the SCM Focus Press book *Superplant: Creating a Nimble Manufacturing Enterprise with Adaptive Planning Software*. The definition of a superplant can be found at this link.

  http://www.scmfocus.com/productionplanningandscheduling/2013/04/22/
  multi-plant-superplant-planning-definition/

Different locations within a superplant have their production lines integrated by shipping portions or increments of their sub-components to an intermediate plant or the finished goods assembly plant. This may occur on a daily basis and is sometimes enabled by a "milk run", integrating the facilities in a circuit. When this design is used, the company has two basic options for how to manage the flow of material.

1. *Use the Truck's Arrival as the Replenishment Trigger:* The first option is to allow the truck's arrival and schedule to control the quantity that is shipped at each stop in the milk run. This has the advantage of allowing the truck to keep a consistent scheduled, and means that receiving plants can generally count on a specific or published arrival time. The factory can then plan their production runs around this time, (although they may have sufficient inventory to keep the line running without adjusting for the truck's schedule). In this scenario, **stock transport orders are created after the count is made at the shipping dock** and the count is variable depending upon what is available. In this case there is no need to pass the stock transport requisition from the planning system to the ERP system. The stock transport requisitions can be visible in the planning system to the planners, but are simply not sent to the ERP system. (This article shows the options for sending requisitions to the ERP system.) In this case the ERP system simply records what has already happened in the factory. The production orders actually control the flows between locations, with the stock movements being controlled by the truck schedule. It is then the responsibility of the transportation department to set up the truck's itinerary to meet the needs of all of the production facilities.

2. *Planning System Stock Transfer Requisition Converted to Stock Transfer Order:* The second option is to allow the supply planning system to initiate the stock transfer order by following the normal process flow of supply planning, with requisitions created in the planning system, which are then converted to stock transport orders either by their transfer to ERP or in the ERP system. However, to follow this approach, an adjustment is necessary to the maximum lot size of the subcomponent so that the production order does not drive the stock transport requisition to be larger than what is desired to be shipped in increments between the factories, and thus breaking the continuous flow of material required to support integrated manufacturing.

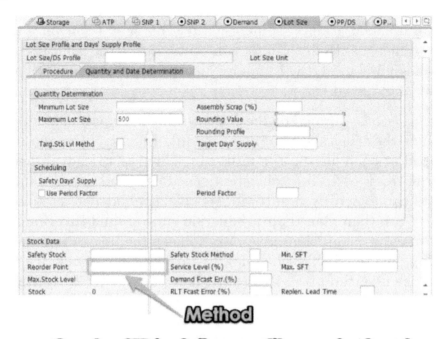

Method

Creates STR in daily quantity required and creates multiple instead of one large STR.

This setting will force the creation of stock transport requisitions in the quantity determined in the maximum lot size field. Because the requirement (initiated by a planned production order) will land on a specific day, this may mean that the system will create all stock transport requisitions on one day. However, the requisitions can be manually spaced out to the days desired.

For two factories that are part of what is in essence one production line, simply shipping what is currently available makes a lot of sense. The truck schedule, rather than the system becomes the pacesetter, which determines the control of material movement. This is with the caveat that the **truck's schedule must be intelligently designed to best synchronize the factories**. This illustrates the principle that for stock movements that are based upon integrated work centers, the natural capacities of the resources take control from the planning system in materials management.

This aso shows that the type of replenishment trigger can depend upon the particular scenario. The method to be used could logically be determined based upon plant proximity. In cases where the plants are within a day or so drive between one another, option 1 could be used. When plants are further away from each other than this, having the supply planning system trigger the movements would make more sense.

Conclusion

This chapter explained the various replenishment triggers that are available to companies both within their supply chain software, as well as outside the software. This entire chapter was designed to serve as a primer on the topic of how triggers are used in order to prepare readers for what is to come. In the next chapter we will see how the different supply planning replenishment triggers are combined for a number of product location combinations in order to create the emergent property of the requirement strategy.

CHAPTER 4

Requirements Strategies

How the forecasts **and orders** are managed or used by the supply planning system is normally referred to as the requirements strategy. One of the complexities of the requirements strategy is that it is assigned within the supply planning system **at each** product location combination. However, when one speaks of a requirements strategy it is easy to lapse into the oversimplified view that a BOM has a single requirements strategy, when in fact, a BOM really has a **combination** of requirements strategies. By combining various requirements strategies in a single BOM, the supply planning application can be made to meet the requirements of various manufacturing environments. In fact, the overall product location database can be thought of as a **matrix**, which is connected through a series of BOMs and each material in each BOM has some requirements strategy assignment that tells the material how to behave. The matrix below shows how BOM assignments can change per PLC or product location combination.

BOM to PLC Assignment

Product Description	Location	Variant	BOM Assignments
Tunafish Sandwich (Standard)	San Diego	1	1
Tunafish Sandwich (Healthy)	San Diego	2	2
Roast Beef Sandwich (Standard)	San Diego	1	3
Roast Beef Sandwich (Healthy)	San Diego	2	4
Cheddar Cheese	San Diego	1	1, 3
Swiss Cheese	San Diego	1	2, 4
Tunafish	San Diego	1	1, 2
Roast Beef	San Diego	1	3, 4
Tomatoes	San Diego	1	1, 2, 3, 4
Spinach	San Diego	1	2, 4
Whole Wheat Bread	San Diego	1	1, 3
White Bread	San Diego	1	2, 4
Mustard	San Diego	1	1, 2, 3, 4
Mayonnaise	San Diego	1	1, 3

This example shows four finished goods and therefore four BOMs for a sandwich shop in San Diego. Each product location combination is part of one of these four BOMs or multiple BOMs.

If we took just one BOM, and limited our manufacturing environments to just two, the matrix would looks something like the following.

Manufacturing Environment Configuration

BOM Level	Material	Reqirements Strategy	
		Make to Stock	Make to Order
1	Finished Good		
2	Component		
3	Raw Material		

Each BOM can only be configured for one manufacturing environment per planning run.

Let's begin with a discussion of just two manufacturing environments. In supply planning one can apply the forecast to different levels of the BOM.

1. *Make to Stock (MTS)*: Uses the forecast for the finished good.

2. *Assemble to Order (ATO):* Uses the forecasts at the component.

In ATO manufacturing environments, the forecast for the finished good is **not relevant** for supply planning, because assemble to order environments do not use a forecast at the finished good level to drive replenishment. This does not mean the forecast is **not** generated, a forecast will probably still be generated by the system – and possibly used for other purposes outside of supply planning.

The Purpose of Forecasting in a ATO Environment

It can be confusing to understand the reason for producing a forecast when the forecast is not used in the supply planning system. A good example of this is reorder point planning. Reorder points do not use a forecast because the replenishment order is created when the stock value falls below the reorder point. In the same way, in ATO environments for finished goods, the trigger for replenishment is not the forecast but an order. Therefore, the purpose of creating a forecast in ATO environments is to apply the forecast at the component and raw material level. The forecast, while generated for the finished good, is simply ignored by the supply planning system.

Understanding the Requirements Strategy

How the forecast is applied is referred to as the requirements strategy in the demand and supply planning system Demand Works Smoothie (and most other supply planning systems). At their essence, requirements strategies control what drives the replenishment. In most cases, the requirement strategies control whether the forecast or the sales order triggers replenishment, but how the forecast is consumed can also play a role. And in some systems, the requirements strategy also controls whether an availability check is performed. I won't get into either of those as this point, as they are tangential to the topic that is currently being discussed. Requirements strategies are a universal feature of supply planning functionality, because there is **always** flexibility required in terms of how the forecast is used by the supply planning system. This is why most supply planning systems can flex between the different manufacturing environments. If we break down the term "requirements strategy," it is simply the strategy for how requirements **percolate** through the supply planning system.

Specific Requirements Strategies

In Demand Works Smoothie,there are **three different** requirements strategies to choose from. Bigger more complex systems, like SAP, often have many more requirements strategies, but upon review, most of these strategies are either very niche or just slight variations to each other.

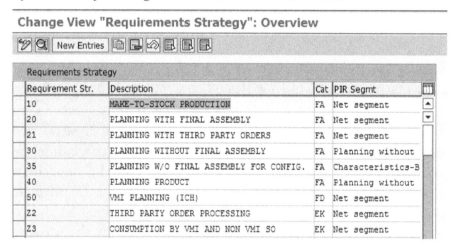

These are the standard requirements strategies in SAP APO.

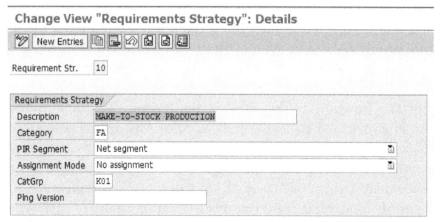

However, each requirements strategy is just a combination of 6 fields. These fields are explained below. The really important fields are actually the fields 2 to 5.

1. *Description:* The name and description.

2. *Category:* The Stock/Receipt/Requirement/Forecast category that is to be as part of the requirements strategy. Only those items processed outside of the supply network (i.e.VMI, Third Party Order Processing) have a category other than forecast in this field.

3. *PIR (Planned Independent Requirements) Segment*: This is the field that specifies the segment for which you want the system to create the planned independent requirement. A planned independent requirement is a demand element – a forecast or a sales order. This is actually a quite involved setting, and I have SAP's definition listed after these bullet points.

4. *Assignment Mode:* Determines how sales orders consume the forecast (referred to as forecast consumption). Only one type of consumption is possible for each requirements strategy. The most common method is to simply have the sales order reduce the forecast.

5. *Category Group: "In forecast consumption you use the category group to determine which kind of orders, for example sales orders or planned orders, can consume the forecast. - SAP Help"* This is simply the demand element. It would be more logical if this field were simply named "demand."

6. *Planning Version:* This is which planning version this requirement strategy applies to. A planning version is a discrete and separate environment. There is one active or live version in SAP APO, and this is the version that sends and receives information from the ERP system. SAP APO, as with many supply chain-planning systems allows for the creation of multiple versions. These versions are often called simulation versions and are used to test a change to the system. One can do whatever one likes in a simulation version without affecting the active or live version. The one thing to consider is that the live versions and the simulation or inactive versions run on the same hardware. Therefore activities which cause a significant amount of processing must be performed when the live system is not also performing significant processing or else the simulation version will take processing cycles from the live version – and may adversely affect the planning output of the live version.

Here we will show some of the complexity that is involved with requirements strategies that are setup in supply planning systems. The example we will use is from SAP's ERP system. What I am about to show I have never seen explained in such a specific way in another documented form. However, I believe SAP's terminology can be translated into a much easier to understand set explanation for each of the important fields of the requirements strategy. Below I have placed what the setting controls next to each of the fields, which SAP uses rather impenetrable names.

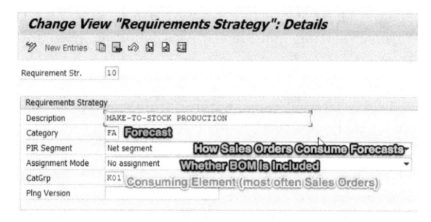

I believe this is far easier to understand than SAP's terminology. This is what the requirements strategy is actually controlling.

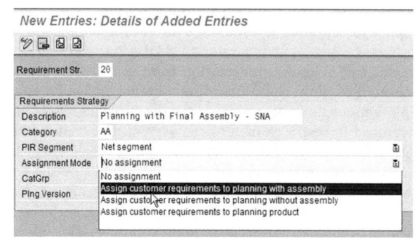

Each of these fields can be changed and, when renamed, **a new requirements strategy can be created.** *Here, in the assignment mode, it is determined when the as-*

signment is made between the customer requirements and a planning strategy, e.g. planning with assembly, planning without assembly or to a planning product or no assignment.[1]

The requirements strategies are always assigned to the product location master. So each product in a BOM has a requirements strategy at each location where the product is carried.

Each requirements strategy is the combination of four primary fields. Although many requirements strategies could be created in SAP APO, the complexity of the requirement strategy options is often much more than meets the eye. Some software vendors try to impress their customers with a long list of requirements strategies, indicating that they can handle many more environments than their competitors.[2] However, after having reviewed the configuration of

---

[1] A planning product is a product that is used for planning purposes – but is often not a real product. It is often a proxy entity that is assigned to a real product, or as is often the case to multiple products. Planning products are often used for aggregated planning in SAP APO.

[2] One of these vendors is SAP. SAP has a long observed approach of just adding functionality that is designed to impress – so they take a "kitchen sink," approach to software de-

the requirements strategies of many companies, I've found that it is very rare to see the more exotic requirements strategies actually used on a project.

Now that we have covered requirements strategies in principle, let's go over the requirements strategies available within Demand Works Smoothie. While it's good to understand the complexity of requirements strategies in a system like SAP, the application Smoothie has much easier to understand requirements strategies.

Requirements Strategies Available within Smoothie

Unlike within SAP APO and SAP ERP, in Demand Works Smoothie, there are only **three** requirements strategies. Rather than stating the requirements strategy in terms of how it fits within a particular manufacturing environment, Smoothie states its requirements strategies in terms of how the product location combination is replenished. I believe this is a significant advantage over systems like SAP that declare the specific manufacturing environment for the requirements strategy. Requirements strategies do not directly map to a specific manufacturing environment, because it is the combination of requirement strategies at each product/location within the BOM or recipe that determines the manufacturing environment setting. The main question to be answered is: when replenishment is scheduled? For a make to order produced finished good, the answer to this question is that every product location combination in the BOM or recipe must wait for a sales order before replenishment is triggered. Each manufacturing environment has a different answer to the question of replenishment for the combination of products and locations in their BOM or recipe. That background is a perfect primer for understanding the requirement strategy settings in Smoothie, as Smoothie has adopted the logic of this paragraph. The following options are available for each product location combination in Smoothie.

---

velopment. Looking at Demand Works' development orientation, they are engineering rather than sales driven in terms of development. Therefore they tend to only put things in the application that are really necessary. This makes the resulting system easier to master and lower in maintenance and it also highlights an engineering approach versus a marketing or sales approach. These types of distinctions are very clear when analyzing different applications in enterprise software, however there is not a very good way for companies to find out about these distinctions from hiring the most popular.

1. *Replenish:* This is the default for every product location combination. This replenishment strategy will perform time-based replenishment, respecting the parameters on the policy tab of the application.

2. *Replenish to Order:* The most common setting — and used for a traditional MTO environment. Demand will equal open orders. This does not use forecasts.

3. *Do Not Replenish:* Sets independent demand to equal open demand orders — forecast not included. It will cancel open supply receipts outside of lead-time. It will not replenish even if ending inventory will go below minimum.[3]

Now lets take a look at **where** the Requirements Strategy is applied within Smoothie.

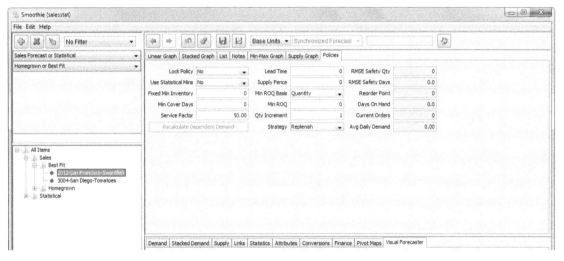

This is the Policies Tab in Smoothie. This is where all of the parameters that control the supply plan are located. The Requirements Strategy is towards the bottom middle of the right pane. It is currently set on "Replenish" because I have not adjusted the default value.

---

[3] Paraphrased from the Demand Works Smoothie Help Documentation – version 7.3.

Assigning Requirements Strategies with Attribute Navigation

Smoothie has an advantage over other supply planning applications; it can use **attributes**, assignments of characteristics to product location combinations, or SKU-Ls to filter products. Smoothie is one of the few planning systems that works this way. Smoothie has taken an approach that was previously only applied to demand planning and leverages it for **supply planning**. This allows the Requirements Strategy, or any other policy value, to be adjusted as part of a mass change. This is one reason why Smoothie is so appropriate for companies with limited maintenance resources.[4]

Here I have selected all product locations under the attribute of Produce. When I change the Requirements Strategy field to Replenish as I have in this screen shot, it changes the Requirements Strategy for all of the product/location combos with this attribute. This could be two product locations or hundreds of product locations. In fact, I can create a custom attribute, which is only used for assigning Requirements Strategies.

The Policies Tab houses supply planning inventory parameters in the application. Any supply planning system really has two dominant control mechanisms.

---

[4] Efficient and transparent alteration of inventory parameters within supply planning systems turns out to be one of the most underestimated areas of functionality within this software category.

1. *The Planning Method:* This is the procedure that is used to calculate the plan. Examples of different methods for supply and production planning are MRP/DRP, cost optimization, and allocation.

2. *The Inventory Parameters:* This includes the values on the Smoothie Policies Tab in the previous screen shot.

Inventory parameters tend to be greatly underemphasized within companies, so they are a primary reason that the application provides far less effective planning output than it should. My work has lead me to conclude that such parameters should be calculated in a way where each parameter is calculated along with other parameters as part of a "package," and that the parameters per product location combination should be cognizant of the parameters values for the other product locations. However, I have never seen a company that works with parameters from this perspective.

Requirements Strategies and the BOM

Now that we have covered the Requirements Strategies, it's necessary to close the loop and see how the Requirements Strategies interact with the BOM and the recipe (for process industry manufacturing).

We can keep the example to a very simple BOM with only three materials. There is really no reason to bring the multiples of raw materials or components per finished good into the scenario because it is an unnecessary complication. Therefore we will simple assume a 1:1 ratio between all the materials in the BOM. So here is my imaginary BOM.

1. *Product A:* Finished Good

2. *Product B:* Component

3. *Product C:* Raw Material

In supply planning systems, every material has a Replenishment Strategy, and how each product is configured with respect to the Replenishment Strategy determines how the overall BOM matches the requirement. To explain this, let's start off with make to stock.

Make to Stock

Here is how we would code the replenishment strategy if we wanted to do MTS:

1. *Product A:* Finished Good: Requirements Strategy = Replenish

2. *Product B:* Subcomponent: Requirements Strategy = Replenish

3. *Product C:* Raw Material: Requirements Strategy = Replenish

Now we have Product A flowing the demand/requirements from the forecasting system to the supply planning system so that the forecast drives the replenishment at the finished good. Although, because Product A is a produced product, what this really means is that production is scheduled **on the basis of the forecast** – rather than as it was in the previous example, on the basis of actual orders.

Make to Order

Here is how we would code the Replenishment Strategy if we wanted to do MTO:

1. *Product A:* Finished Good: Requirements Strategy = Replenish to Order

2. *Product B:* Component: Requirements Strategy = Replenish to Order

3. *Product C:* Raw Material: Requirements Strategy = Replenish to Order

Product A, the finished good, is not replenished on the basis of the forecast. Because it is a produced material, and not a procured material, it does not schedule a production order until a sales order comes through the system. However, Product B and Product C are set to replenish to order, so they work the same way. This means that no component and raw material will be ready or in stock when the sales order comes through, and there will also be procurement lead time, which, under most circumstances, is far longer, and has higher variability versus manufacturing lead time. As one can see, for most make to order products, the customer must be willing to wait.

In the next example, ATO, the Requirements Strategies will need to be adjusted. Again, the forecast is still generated for each product in the BOM, but the Requirements Strategies changes **the application** of the forecast.

Assemble to Order

Here is how we would code the Replenishment Strategy if we wanted to do make to order:

1. *Product A:* Finished Good: Requirements Strategy = Replenish to Order

2. *Product B:* Component: Requirements Strategy = Replenish

3. *Product C:* Raw Material: Requirements Strategy = Replenish

Product A, the finished good, is not replenished on the basis of the forecast. Because it is a produced material, and not a procured material, it does not have a production order scheduled for it **until a sales order comes through the system**. However, Product B and Product C are set to replenish, so they do work off of the forecast, which means they have to have their own forecast as they cannot rely upon a planning bill of materials explosion to create purchase requisitions.

This means that the component and raw material **will be ready** when the sales order comes through, and there will be **no procurement lead time**, which under most circumstances is far longer, and has higher variability versus manufacturing lead time.

Engineer to Order

As was discussed in Chapter 2: Introduction to Different Manufacturing Environments, ETO does not fit with how supply planning systems work because neither the forecast nor the sales order is used to trigger either production or procurement. Sub components and raw material can be procured in stages. Therefore, the most logical approach to setting the requirements strategies is to simply set all of the materials in the BOM or recipe to "Do Not Replenish." This way the replenishment can be triggered manually for all of the products.

1. *Product A:* Finished Good: Requirements Strategy = Do Not Replenish

2. *Product B:* Subcomponent: Requirements Strategy = Do Not Replenish

3. *Product C:* Raw Material: Requirements Strategy = Do not Replenish

Multiple Production Environments

The other manufacturing environments such as engineer to order (ETO) or build to order (BTO) are essentially variants of assemble to order.[5] However, with these manufacturing environments there is more postponement in how components are replenished. For instance a BTO/MTO BOM might look like the following:

BTO/MTO

1. *Product A:* Finished Good: Requirements Strategy = Do Not Replenish

2. *Product B:* Subcomponent: Requirements Strategy = Do Not Replenish

3. *Product C:* Raw Material: Requirements Strategy = Replenish

There is often the concept that a supply planning system must be specifically designed to meet the requirements of a manufacturing environment. However, I have not found this to be the case. By setting different Requirements Strategies throughout the individual product location combinations through the various BOMs, most supply planning systems should be able to meet the requirements of different manufacturing environments all within one application.

Conclusion

Requirements Strategies are one of the more confusing areas of supply planning, and many consultants have a hard time explaining how requirements strategies work – but requirements strategies can be simplified when following is understood:

1. They are the **primary linchpin** between the forecasting system and the supply planning system.

2. They determine how the forecast is used by the supply planning system.

Requirements strategies have three primary functions:

1. Determine **how** the forecast is applied to supply planning.

---

[5] I am very much a fan of the definitions of BTO and MTO at Arena Solutions. http://www. arenasolutions.com/resources/articles/engineered-to-order

2. Determine **when** replenishment is scheduled.

3. In the case of finished goods, or a components internally produced by a company – determines when production is scheduled.

4. Determine the **level of planning** of the BOM. That is if the finished good is not produced without an order (make to order) then the planning level in the BOM is at the component. When the finished good is produced to a forecast, (make to stock) the planning level is higher – at the finished good.

How the forecasts **and orders** are managed or used by the supply planning system is normally referred to as the requirements strategy. In assemble to order manufacturing environments, the forecast at the finished good is **not relevant** for supply planning, because assemble to order environments do not use a forecast at the finished good level to drive replenishment. This does not mean the forecast is **not** generated, a forecast will probably still be generated by the system – and possibly used for other purposes outside of supply planning. At their essence, requirements strategies control what drives the replenishment. The requirements strategies must be set to model the manufacturing environment or manufacturing environments of the company. This chapter explained how each requirement strategy in two different applications would be set to model the each manufacturing environment.

Now we will move on to a common misunderstanding regarding manufacturing strategies or what I call the make to order illusion.

CHAPTER 5

The Make to Order Illusion

I have noticed, in my consulting practice, that many executives tell me that they would eventually like to move from an MTS to an MTO environment. I believe there are a number of misunderstandings with respect to what qualifies as an MTO environment. This will be the topic of this chapter.

The Motivations of Moving to Make to Order

There are several motivations for companies that desire to move to an MTO environment:

- The desire to seem leading-edge.

- The desire to remove the company from the complexities of performing forecasting, or to eliminate bad forecasting.

- The adaptation of 'LEAN' principles, which is the movement to carrying very low inventories and removing waste

- All of the above motivations can be boiled down to a single core goal: find a magic bullet that will solve a company's planning problems. Obviously, any company that could move to an MTO environment would never have to forecast, never have to keep inventory and would not have waste in the form of products that are obsolesced before they can be sold. It would also eliminate the need to reposition stock (called **redeployment**). Sounds great!

However, whether a company can be successful in an MTO environment has little to do with what the executives in the company would like, and is primarily dependent on the market the company is in and the type of product that they sell. What is often unmentioned is whether the company in question exists in an environment where customers **are willing to wait** for their items to be produced, or if they expect them to be available when they want them. Is the customer's lead-time expectation longer or shorter than the total supply chain lead-time? In the vast majority of cases, the customer lead-time is **shorter** than the supply chain lead-time, rendering discussions of moving to an MTO manufacturing environment a moot point (unless the company enjoys bad customer service feedback and falling sales!). Furthermore, what is often left out of discussions related to make-to-order is the increase in cost that frequently results from an MTO environment. Long production runs are cost efficient, while shorter runs are less efficient. Therefore "mating" the production process to demand completely changes the economics of manufactured products. Making your products to order means only procuring input products after a sales order has been created. Therefore this generally means less procurement efficiency with smaller order sizes, and more expensive shipping and handling of the procured product (not to mention higher prices for the consumer, and thus, lower sales in competitive markets).

The Relationship between Make to Order and the Product's Margin

Most MTO environments deal in high margin products. Lockheed Martin works in a high margin business. While pricing fluctuates wildly, the latest estimates of the price paid by the US government for the F-35 fighter is $219 million. Ferrari makes all of its cars to order. Ferraris cost roughly $200,000. Certainly, some of the cost is the premium materials used, but some of the cost is related to the manufacturing inefficiency, which is directly traceable to the MTO model. This is explained in the following quotation.

*"All that go-fast goodness, and the aura that comes with it, will
cost you. A brand new Ferrari California would set you back
around $192,000 as of mid-2010. One reason is that they don't come
streaming off the assembly line every few minutes like the typical
Toyota or Ford models do. Despite modern manufacturing and
efficiency practices, Ferraris aren't made exactly like mass-market
vehicles."*

– How Long to Build a Ferrari

The total build time of a Ferrari is roughly 30 days; however, this is not the order cycle time. A typical customer will wait 1 to 2 years for their Ferrari to arrive. Some of this is simply having too much demand for the production capacity – however, the upshot of this is that Ferrari buyers wait a long time for their purchases to arrive. The company gets away with this by courting high-end clientele who don't mind the wait to get 'the best'.

Lockheed Martin and Ferrari are highly differentiated in the market and have very high margins. However, not all companies are in high margin businesses or so differentiated or in such special markets. Most, in fact, are not; and these companies generally need to be cost competitive, so the extra costs associated with MTO is not typically going to be acceptable.

The Extra Costs of Make to Order vs. Make to Stock Environments:

- Increased transportation costs (to get suppliers to the company faster)

- Increased change-overs on machinery

- Increased costs of supplies, both in higher ordering costs per item, and higher transportation costs as smaller orders lead to higher per unit transportation costs.

- Decreased utilization of factory equipment (as equipment must wait for input material, which may be late or on route when the equipment is ready to produce)

- Rush jobs that can both reduce the quality of the accepted items, and produce more finished goods that must be scrapped. This means that more raw material must be purchased for every sellable item.

Considering the Total Costs and Quality Implications

Overall, while moving a make to stock environment to make to order, the company reduces its planning, but increases its costs and reduces its product quality. This **should be considered evidence** that supply chain planning adds value to the overall supply chain process.

Companies may be frustrated with their planning results, but when they describe moving to an MTO environment, even in situations where it is feasible to transition to make to order planning, the executives in companies generally **do not add up** all the extra costs and problems that come from producing in this way. This leads to the next point, which is what executives often mean when the talk about moving to an MTO manufacturing environment.

In fact, in the haste to move to make to order environments, companies often use examples of "make to order" environments that **are not in fact make to order (with modifications at the finishing line)**. Forecasting is still necessary. Two examples of environments that are called make to order, but are not, are listed below.

Assemble to Order Example 1: Computers

For instance, they may bring up Dell Computers, a company well-known for their online business not building the entire computer, but instead holding components and then building on demand once an order is received. As long as all the components are in stock, a computer can be assembled quickly. This is how Dell has stayed away from creating final products, which would mean they would have to guess or forecast as to how many of each configuration would be required.[1] However, this is not make to order. Manufacturing environments

---

[1] In fact, Dell did many things right with respect to supply chain management, and assemble to order was only one of them. Dell was one of the early innovators in demand shaping and sales and operations planning. For instance, Dell salespeople would steer customers to configurations for which they had all of the components that they could immediately build. This is a form of demand shaping and is not specific to assemble to order.

The descriptions of Dell in its heyday describe a level of cooperation between sales, marketing and operations that I have never seen in a company. For whatever reason, the focus on Dell has tended to be on their assemble to order model. However, there were actually sev-

that people call "make to order" are actually "assemble to order." However, assemble to order **still requires a forecast at the subcomponent level**. This is why companies must forecast. Dell has a type of product where the complexity really resides in the components, and the assembly of the components is the easy part. Therefore, they defer the easy part until they receive a firm order. Interestingly, more OEMs have become assembly operations rather than integrated manufacturing operations. A perfect example of this is the automobile manufacturing industry where much of the complexity of the manufacturing of automobiles has been decentralized to suppliers. Most of the OEMs (Ford, Toyota, etc.) now receive complex assemblies (dashboards, engines, etc.) from suppliers and only serve to assemble them – meaning that most of the actual manufacturing complexity now resides with suppliers rather than the OEM. This actually increases the company's ability to move to a make to order manufacturing environment.

Assemble to Order Example 2: Books

If we take the example of book production, many companies are at the point where they can produce one book at a time. This is called print on demand or POD, and one well-known company that does this is Lightning Source.

Prior to books being purchased online, there was little need for print on demand as books were purchased from bookstores, and while a book could always be special ordered the majority of books were purchased from stock on hand. However, with the massive growth of Amazon as well as other online booksellers, make to order became increasingly feasible from the market perspective – and it turns out that it also became feasible from the manufacturing perspective. Companies perfected the ability to create books in batches of one. This is highly advantageous because inventory management has always been the bane of bookmakers. In fact, prior to the development of online book buying, the limitations of inventory management greatly restricted the number of titles that could be carried and sold. In this environment much of the power was with the book publishers who served as brokers for what would be published and what would not be – which greatly limited the number of books that could

---

eral factors, and several that were specific to supply chain management, that lead to Dell's success.

be published. Online book selling moved the leverage to the book seller – notably Amazon.com.

The combination of online book selling with print on demand has transformed book publishing with many more titles carried than ever before. Of course, the rise of electronic books such as the Kindle platform has increased the diversity of books even more than POD – but, as Kindle is an electronic medium, it does not fall into the topic of supply chain management. If a Kindle electronic book is published, the interaction is simply the downloading of a file between the book seller's server and the customer's computer. There is, in this case, no supply chain, as it is a simple file transfer.

Print on demand is quite impressive, and means that authors and publishers do not have to engage in long production runs, which is particularly important during the early stages of a book's life when its future demand is very hard to predict. However, POD is only possible at a higher unit price, and at a lower quality level. So, even with a simple product that has a very limited supply chain (print pages, bind pages in a press, add cover, repeat), there are still tradeoffs. But more importantly, this still isn't MTO. They don't wait to buy ink and paper until a book is ordered – they buy the paper and ink and hold a stock, meaning they still need to forecast how much paper and ink they'll need.

Using Make to Order Where it Fits

None of this should be misconstrued as criticism of appropriate uses of make to order manufacturing – when the conditions are right employing a make to order environment can be the right fit. And many companies should be MTO, BTO, or ETO. However, the fact remains that many companies that are not in fact appropriate for a **make to order** manufacturing environment spend time dreaming about how they could move to a make to order environment. I have seen companies on the very extreme end of make to stock, such as those in what is referred to as repetitive manufacturing, talk about moving to a make order environment. A repetitive manufacturing environment relies upon high volume and relatively uninterrupted production runs performed on very expensive equipment that costs a lot to maintain or replace. This is not going to be a good environment for MTO production.

Conclusion

It is not possible for the vast majority of companies to move to a build-to-order environment. Except for extremely specialized manufacturing (such as print-on-demand publishing), it's difficult to come up with examples of products that cost the same to produce whether making one or a hundred or a thousand. Companies that actually do operate a make to order manufacturing environment tend to deal in high margin. Similar limitations that are related to manufacturing apply to procurement, as procuring in larger batches is less expensive than procuring in smaller batches.

CHAPTER 6

The Limitations to the Concept of Mass Customization

There are a number of books that propose moving towards increasing customization.[1] Probably the best-known proponent of mass customization is Joseph Pine, author of the book *Mass Customization: The New Frontier in Business Competition*. This is certainly not a new trend; Joseph's book was published back in 1992. This is the type of material that comes up on TED talks, is published in the Harvard Business Review, and is most appealing to those that know the least about true manufacturing constraints. Joseph Pine's basic proposal is as follows:

---

[1] Mass customization is explained in the following way *"Mass customization means that the customer is driving the configured order from a predefined menu, much like what you see in a restaurant, that puts some limits or parameters around what the company is offering to the marketplace,"* adds Gardner. *"A product configurator is usually presented to the customer that specifies what goes with what and what is permissible to be ordered."* – Assembly Magazine

1. *Commoditization*: Manufactured products (in addition to services) have become commoditized

2. *Overwhelming Price Competition*: Therefore the only thing that differentiates them is price.

3. *Shift to Experience Economy*: That differentiation is based upon experience, or how consumers experience the product or service.

Joseph Pine's proposal, and other proponents of mass customization is not actually supported with broad analysis, and mostly relies upon anecdotes that have a very weak connection to manufacturing. For example, there has been a drive to lower prices for products in the US, with a corresponding decline in product quality. This is the so-called Wal-Martization of the economy, but this is **not based upon mass customization**, rather it is based upon outsourced manufacturing and a general reduction in manufacturing standards combined with increased income inequality – particularly in the US.

> *Tony's old pair of Levi's may well have been made in the U.S,*
> *and they likely cost more than his new pair. The new ones were*
> *manufactured abroad — Levi's closed its last U.S. factory in 2003*
> *— and, though Tony didn't buy them at Walmart, their shoddy*
> *construction can be blamed at least in part on the giant retailer and*
> *the way it's reshaping manufacturing around the world.*

> *Since 1994, the consumer price of apparel, in real terms, has fallen*
> *by 39 percent. "It is now possible to buy clothing, long a high-priced*
> *and valuable commodity, by the pound, for prices comparable to*
> *cheap agricultural products," notes Juliet Schor. Cheapness — and*
> *the decline in durability that has accompanied it — has triggered*
> *an astonishing increase in the amount of clothing we buy. In the*
> *mid-1990s, the average American bought 28 items of clothing a year.*
> *Today, we buy 59 items. We also throw away an average of 83 pounds*
> *of textiles per person, mostly discarded apparel, each year. That's*
> *four times as much as we did in 1980, according to an EPA analysis*
> *of municipal waste streams. Prices on general household goods have*
> *fallen by about one-third since the mid-1990s. Given how awash in*
> *stuff we were in those boom years, it's shocking just how much more*

we buy now. Since 1995, the number of toasters and other small
electro-thermal appliances sold in the U.S. each year increased from
188 million to 279 million. The average household now buys a new
TV every 2.5 years, up from every 3.4 years in the early 1990s. We buy
more than 2 billion bath towels a year, up from 1.4 billion in 1994.
— Is Your Stuff Falling Apart?

This is a trend based not upon mass customization, but based upon outsourced manufacturing and lowered product reliability and longevity, which is clearly evident. Products made in countries like China or Vietnam are less expensive and have more product defects and lower lifespans, and this trend overwhelms any trend towards more product customization, but it's not particularly aspirational, so it won't get admitted into any TED talks or Harvard Business Review articles.

Essentially, these type of books propose that companies can both produce in large quantities and produce customized output. However, most of the examples provided by the book *Custom Nation: Why Customization Is the Future of Business and How to Profit From It* aren't even manufacturing environments, nor are the products produced truly custom. Of examples provided in the book which include Paris Miki, Chipotle and Netflix. Paris Miki – a high end Japanese eyewear retailer – specializes in 'custom' frames, but the customization is minimal, in terms of functionality. Chipotle, where the burrito is "made to order", is a fast food chain with bought-in prepared food that is combined as the customer likes (think back, was there ever a time where food offered in restaurants could not be adjusted by simply asking?)[2]. Netflix provides streaming movies and television programs and a mail-order DVD service, the physical

---

[2] Not to be overly detail oriented, but a burrito would be assemble to order as the raw materials are already sitting there in trays. A burrito that is build to order would mean that the input materials were not yet purchased and stocked, and that when arriving in Chipotle, you would describe the ingredients that you wanted in your burrito and the order taker would then go across the street and buy the ingredients and then come back and cook the meet, slice the tomatoes, open the cheese package. In a build to order environment, the input materials are not purchased until the sales order is created. This is why build to order environments are so rare and also why there will never be a build to order burrito restaurant.

part of what Netflix does is a warehousing operations, not a manufacturing operation. That is an important distinction, because to start a conversation about customized manufacturing and then to provide examples which are not manufacturing is the very definition of a misleading argument. They also happen to be examples where the producer is direct to the consumer. There is little relevance here between what these companies do and the majority of manufacturers. Examples that are provided are often high-end luxury items that can afford very high levels of production inefficiency. Certainly a high end-racing bicycle can be made in a customized fashion, and customized manufacturing has always existed, but there is nothing new here. One true manufacturing example provided by Joseph Pine is Planters Company.

> *The Planters Company, a unit of Nabisco, chose cosmetic customization when it retooled its old plant in Suffolk, Virginia, in order to satisfy the increasingly diverse merchandising demands of its retail customers. Wal-Mart wanted to sell peanuts and mixed nuts in larger quantities than Safeway or 7-Eleven did, and Jewel wanted different promotional packages than Dominick's did. In the past, Planters could produce only long batches of small, medium, and large cans; as a result, customers had to choose from a few standard packages to find the one that most closely met their requirements. Today the company can quickly switch between different sizes, labels, and shipping containers, responding to each retailer's desires on an order-by-order basis.*
>
> – Harvard Business Review

There is certainly nothing wrong with what Planters did in this example, but what is described is a mixing operation. Planters brings in various nut types into the factory in bulk and then mixes them with each finished good being either a single nut type or a combination of nuts (100% peanuts, peanuts + cashews + almonds, cashews + raisins, etc..), and this is then sent to packaging. This is one of the simplest manufacturing operations that exists, and changing over between the nut types is much lower-cost than, say, mixing paint, where there is a cleanout phase when a lighter color follows a darker color, etc. On the packaging side, Planters clearly needed to purchase more packaging sizes, but one can change the packaging work stations while keeping the mixing operation continuing to run, a packaging changeover does not necessitate a mixing operation changeover in this case. Finally, this change undoubtedly increased production costs and, given the sales potential, it may have been warranted (or may not have been — as no numbers are provided). However, this scenario should not be presented as if there were no costs involved in this change. In fact, this is the thing I noticed about every one of the mass customization examples brought forward in this book, there are no details as to what was required to make the change and what the costs were. Every change is presented as cost-free. Other examples provided by Joseph Pine are horribly simplistic, and would lead to very detrimental effects for companies that implemented them. As an example, in the HBR article, Joseph Pine writes:

> *Inventory is built in anticipation of potential, yet uncertain, demand.*
> *Forecasting becomes the critical activity; but, as everyone knows, even*
> *the best forecasting models fall short. Even if most companies can*
> *accurately forecast their total finished-goods-inventory requirements,*
> *they always err in their projections of exactly which goods will*
> *be needed at which locations and at what times. Collaborative*
> *customizers, in contrast, minimize costs by not keeping inventories*
> *of finished products. Instead, they stock raw materials or component*
> *parts and then make finished products only in response to the actual*
> *needs of individual customers. They transport a given product only to*
> *those places where they know it is needed.*
> — The Four Faces of Customization

I work in forecasting, and this is really a terribly simplistic explanation of forecasting. Certainly all forecasts contain inaccuracy; however, forecasts are necessary because there is a lead-time that is required for obtaining input material, production, and moving the material through the outbound supply chain. It is certainly advantageous to keep inventories in finished products to a minimum by running ATO, or planning without final assembly, but not all products are amenable to this mode of production and distribution. It will not be feasible for lightbulbs to be stocked at the assembly level and for the factory to initiate manufacturing on a small batch of light bulbs. Any company that operated this way would have to charge such a high price for light bulbs that they would be quickly out of business. On top of that, most goods in the manufacturing world still must be sold on store shelves or offered with a supply of finished stock before demand is known because consumers don't recognize a need for them until they are given the opportunity to make a purchase (this means the demand lead-time is near zero, but the supply lead-time is large!).

It is frustrating to me, as a professional in this field, because Joseph Pine is writing in the Harvard Business Review, graduated from MIT, is considered by many a thought leader and does not understand elementary supply chain constraints, or knows them and is simply leading people down this garden path in order to sell books and consulting.

Some of the logic for moving towards a make to order environment is actually circular, but one has to dig a little bit in order to understand why. For instance, there is a claim that with so many products being offered by so many companies, it is less feasible to have long production runs – as demand is increasingly spread over more products. This makes forecasting more difficult, reducing the incentives to carry the inventory necessary to support the production runs of a traditional length. Therefore the answer, promoted by mass customization supporters, is to **move more towards make to order manufacturing**. However, what is not discussed is why demand is now spread over so many products. In some cases it is authentic demand, but in other cases there has been product proliferation that has been driven by marketing and many of the actual product differences are quite small or illusory. A review of the toothpaste isle at your supermarket is a good example of this.

Most of these toothpaste containers contain essentially a similar to identical set of chemical compounds; however, marketing provides customers with different varieties of what is often the same product in order to promote purchases. Many of the claims are unfounded, but because there is very little regulation (in the US at least), one can say what they like regarding what the toothpaste will do for consumers. Whether promotional material on the packaging is true or not is barely mentioned, and anyone who might bring this up is considered hopelessly naïve as the primary focus is whether or not the claim will increase sales.

> *"Retailers are faced by increasing assortment. In grocery retail, product life cycles have been decreasing. As a consequence, it is increasingly difficult to forecast sales for an individual item in a particular store for tactical reasons, as time series tend to be short. Moreover, retail sales are faced with extensive promotion activities. Products are typically on promotion for a limited period of time, e.g. one week during which demand is usually substantially higher than during periods without promotion, and many stock outs occur during promotions due to inaccurate forecasts."*
> – SKU Demand Forecasting in the Presence of Promotions

Marketing, in an effort to justify its value to manufacturers, has greatly increased the number of products that are carried. However, marketing does not want to be held responsible for the naturally increased costs of producing so many different items, or spreading similar demand levels over far more products. Therefore, it attempts to redirect the issue to being one that is squarely placed onto operations. Marketing could introduce fewer products, and actually increase the companies' profitability, but it **chooses** not to for its own internal reasons that have nothing or, at least very little, to do with the benefits to the company as a whole. A primary reason for this is the motivation of marketing, which is based upon demonstrating its value through new product introduction, and or changing the terms of the sale of the existing items – generally referred to as promotions. The end result is that others must adjust around Marketing, regardless of the business outcomes. In the case of promotions, a primary Marketing focal point, as explained in the SCM Focus Press book *Promotions Forecasting: Forecast Adjustment Techniques in Software*, is in overstating the benefits of promotions to the rest of the company. Considering the popularity of promotions, the evidence for them is quite mixed, and non-sales and non-marketing executives often take it for granted that the benefits of promotions are quite substantial. However, once one looks at the actual research into promotions, the benefits are far less clear than assumed.

> *"So do price promotions pay off? To answer that question, we analyzed seven years of scanner data, covering 25 product categories and 75 brands, from the Chicago area's second-largest supermarket chain, Dominick's Finer Foods. Previous research showed that price chain, Dominick's Finer Foods. Previous research showed that price promotions tend to have little long-term effect on sales volume. Our new research found that the same is true for revenues and margins: They quickly snap back to baseline. But in the short-to-medium term, promotions can have very strong positive and negative effects that can hit retailers and manufacturers in very different ways."*
>
> – Who Benefits from Price Promotions?

The costs of promotions, whether those costs are front-end or back-end, typically are not quantified within companies. Often, promotions are not even compared with other expenditures such as normal advertising, although there is evidence that they really should be. A survey of U.S. companies has shown that those companies that spent 60 percent of their total budget on promotions underperformed companies that spent most of their budget on advertising instead of promotions.

The other big marketing tool is in new product development. In case anyone questions the validity of the statement regarding the actual benefit to the company brought by so many new products, this is explained very well and, in fact, quantified in the book *Islands of Profit in a Sea of Red Ink*.

> *"Nearly every company is 30 to 40 percent unprofitable by any measure. In almost every company, 20 to 30 percent of the business is highly profitable, and a large proportion of this profitability is going to cross-subsidize the unprofitable part of the business. The rest of the company is marginal. The most current metrics and control systems (budgets, etc.) do not even show the problem or the opportunity for improvement."*
>
> — Islands of Profit in a Sea of Red Ink

> *"Some managers argue that it is a good idea to accept business that contributes, even marginally, to covering overhead. However, when you take on a lot of business that contributes only marginally to overhead, in almost all cases it will absorb a significant amount of sales and operations resources that otherwise would have been devoted to increasing your "good" business. And it will remain and grow into the embedded profitability that drags down earnings in company after company."*
>
> — Islands of Profit in a Sea of Red Ink

Product Proliferation

Product proliferation is the increase in the number of products that are carried. Often, the marketing differences between the products are only incidental and illusory. Proliferation would be even worse than it currently is, but retailers only have so much space to offer.

Whose interests does it actually serve to have so many similar products? Does it serve the interests of the company to have so many highly similar products

– does it actually pay for the company to incur all of the extra costs of dealing with the complexity of so many different products, or does this merely serve the interests of marketing (or the retailer)? The question should be asked rather than simply accepting the fact that all product proliferation is good for business. Because of their incentives, both Sales and Marketing are biased towards maximizing revenue – however, the company is actually supposed to be maximizing **profit**. This is the problem – when you create incentives for groups that are entirely focused on maximizing sales, it is quite predictable that the company will metastasize into areas that are not profitable.

The Real Problem with Forecast Accuracy

Another reason listed for moving towards shorter production runs is that many companies have so much difficulty forecasting. However, again, this also tends to be uncritically accepted by proponents of mass customization.

The truth is that companies tend to degrade their demand history through engaging in promotions and pushing sales in order to meet end of quarter sales goals. In every instance that I have reviewed in companies, the variability of the sales history greatly exceeds the variability of the authentic order pattern. Also, as I have discussed in my books on forecasting, companies refuse to invest sufficiently in forecasting, preferring to allocate that money to Sales and Marketing. It is, in fact, very rare for a company to provide a good salary to those that work in supply chain forecasting, aside from the managers and directors. Consulting companies most often recommend forecasting software that is a poor fit for their customers – but can help them maximize their billing hours. This is covered in the following article.

http://www.scmfocus.com/demandplanning/2010/09/why-companies-are-selecting-the-wrong-supply-chain-demand-planning-systems/

This picture is quite a bit different than the one painted by proponents of mass customization – who tend to imply that all of the issues with forecast accuracy are simply related to the market. Some of this sounds very close to the statement "because we lack supply chain management competence, we need to move towards shorter production runs."

Imposing Costs on Operations

Most sales and marketing types, as well as many strategy consultants (none of whom are supply chain experts by the way), propose that extra complexity added by sales and marketing should not be a problem, and that supply chain should simply adapt to more product proliferation and all other complexities introduced by Sales and Marketing. Advanced planning software and optimizers, and advanced forecasting algorithms can manage these issues. Either that, or they propose that "Lean" can do it; whatever the complexity, there is—according to them—a special magic box that can make an inefficient business model design all better. Unknown to many consultants, the less forecastable a product, the less useful (not more useful) advanced methods become. Extremely lumpy products may as well be placed on reorder point planning. Reorder point planning requires no forecast and creates orders on the basis of falling below an inventory level, which is how planning was performed before MRP was introduced. The less erratic the sales history, the more forecastable the PLC, and the more a forecasting system can do with the history—the exact opposite of those who propose that complex solutions can solve the problems of poor planning.

Mass customization – i.e. shorter production runs – is another rallying cry on the part of Sales and Marketing which can help the company manage its strategy. However, is this correct? Is it beneficial for the company for Sales and Marketing to set the entire strategy of the company in terms of what is offered and what is carried at each location and then just have operations meet whatever requirements Sales and Marketing sets forth? Companies routinely discuss having a sales and operations process where Sales/Marketing, Finance and Operations are all equal partners at the table in determining the strategy – however that type of cooperation, which was common at Dell at one time, is absent from most other companies. Sales and Marketing has always proposed shorter production runs under one term or another, with the new fashionable term being "flexible manufacturing." Sales and marketing are normally not concerned with the cost of production because they are not held accountable for anything but revenue growth.

Unrealistic Expectations

While reading books on mass customization, I came across a number of concerning statements that are contradictory to the rules of supply chain management. This one sticks out:

> *"The result of applying mass customization principles include the*
> *reduction of the overall delivery time from 400 to 16 days. Regardless*
> *of the product category or industry, they have all turned customers'*
> *heterogeneous needs into an opportunity to create value, rather*
> *than a problem to be minimized, challenging the "one size fits all"*
> *assumption of traditional mass production."*
>
> – Mass Customization: How to Build to Order, Assemble to
> Order, Configure to Order, Make to Order, and Engineer to
> Order Manufacturers Increase

Firstly, if a company had an overall delivery time of four hundred days that could have been reduced to 16 days, then what performance level was being applied in the first place? And realistically, this sounds like a made up example, because it is such an extreme improvement. If we take a more realistic example, it may be true that delivery time can be reduced, but typically this is not without additional cost. I have worked with many manufacturers and there simply is not the opportunity to reduce overall delivery time – without increasing costs somewhere along the way. However, if the costs are left out of the equation then the picture that is being communicated is not a complete one. As for the second part of the quotation, challenging "one size fits all" manufacturing sounds good, but it's unclear who would be challenged – as I am not aware of anyone who proposes that manufacturing should be "one size fits all." This is an example of a paper tiger argument, where the author creates a fictitious argument that no one proposes, and then knocks it down. What **is proposed** is that there are costs associated with smaller production batch sizes. That has always been true, and will also be true in the future. Longer production runs lead to **both lower unit costs and higher quality**. The quality portion of the previous sentence may be surprising to many people as it is rarely mentioned, but it is a fact. It is well known that the product produced at the beginning of a production run, or when any change is made to the production run is of lower quality because it takes some time to "tune" the manufacturing process. At this point one might presume that this is where statistical process control can improve things, but statistical process control can only tell you if a production batch meets or does not meet a production standard, and whether that batch has a particular probability of being representative of the population produced, it does not help tune the machines in order to reduce the defect level. Shorter production runs will normally lead to either still sellable product or product that must be either scrapped or remanufactured (as well as to less overall volume being produced due to the production time lost to the changeover as well as the tuning phase). Once a production run has been tuned, it can normally run continuously, maintaining a high quality level. This is why such high output levels are reached in repetitive manufacturing things like light bulbs. Repetitive (long production run discrete) and continuous (long production run process) manufacturing are good examples because, too often, the type of production which is proposed for short production runs provide examples from discrete manufacturing, where the costs of shorter production runs are still high, but lower than in other types of manufacturing. Let us review the production categorizations.

The manufacturing categories could be referred to this way:

1. Non-Dis-assemble-able / Short: Discrete

2. Non-Dis-assemble-able / Long: Repetitive

3. Dis-assemble-able / Short: Batch

4. Dis-assemble-able / Long: Continuous

In fact, one could extend the category to include very small production quantities as I have done below:

Production Planning Categorization

	Single Item Production	Short	Long
Disasseble-able	Job Shop	Discrete	Repetitive
Not Disassemble-able	Small Batch	Batch	Continuous

Continuous versus batch manufacturing processes apply to both products that can be disassembled into their original components and to products that cannot. One common approach to segmenting process manufacturing is by whether it is continuous or in batches.

Production Planning Categorization

Length of Production Run

	Short	Long
Yes	Discrete	Repetitive
No	Batch	Continuous

Products Can be Disassembled Into Their Components

When one analyzes the manufacturing categories, its apparent that process industry manufacturing is divided into batch and continuous, and that these categories correlate to discrete and repetitive, but the differentiation is whether the finished good can be disassembled after production into its component parts.

Continuous Production

Continuous process manufacturing means that production doesn't stop for extremely long intervals. Its efficiency advantages are described below:

> *"Shutting down and starting up many continuous processes typically results in off quality product that must be reprocessed or disposed of. Many tanks, vessels and pipes cannot be left full of materials because of unwanted chemical reactions, settling of suspended materials or crystallization or hardening of materials. Also, cycling temperatures and pressures from starting up and shutting down certain processes (line kilns, blast furnaces, pressure vessels, etc.) may cause metal fatigue or other wear from pressure or thermal cycling."*
>
> – Wikipedia

Some continuous processes run for years. The costs in starting and stopping the process are frequently quite high. With continuous manufacturing processes, the efficiency gained from the process is so high that the emphasis is around keeping the process continually working. This means that work shifts must be 24/7. It also means that input materials must be in ready supply and always available, even if that means carrying significant buffer stocks of material.

The Blast Furnace

The first example of this is the blast furnace. Blast furnaces produce metals, and are enormous, and the technology goes back 2000 years, although it was not diffused broadly until the 13th century.

This is a blast furnace. The enormous pipe which connects to the top of the blast furnace carries coke, limestone flux and iron ore to the top of the blast furnace where it is

dropped into the furnace. The furnace itself is tall and cylindrical, with the bottom of the blast furnace being the hottest and the top being the coolest. Hot air is blasted into the side in order to maintain the combustion. Iron is removed from the bottom of the blast furnace.

Obviously this is not the type of manufacturing that would be turned on and off. The blast furnace maintains the highest efficiency when it is run continuously. In fact, according to the Steelworks website, the blast furnace is typically run continuously for between 4 to 10 years. Some methods of production that, at one point, were done in batches could be converted to a more continuous operation through improvements to process control; there are multiple examples of this in the history of both chemical and petroleum refining. In fact, while in discrete manufacturing the trends are to attempt to create "flexible" manufacturing scenarios which result in shorter production runs and more changeovers, in process industry manufacturing the emphasis is to move from batch production to continuous production. However, the restrictions that exist on changing over the blast furnace are listed clearly above. How would a proponent of mass customization propose moving towards shorter production runs for the blast furnace? Let's move on to another example.

Textiles

Another industry that deploys continuous manufacturing is textiles. One often thinks of textiles as simply the assembly of textiles into clothing, automotive seat covers, etc. Those jobs are labor intensive. However, the creation of the textile material is in fact quite automated.

This is an enormous loom, which runs in a continuous fashion. These looms are scaled up and more sophisticated versions of the foot-treadle loom shown below:

Weaving was once a manual activity and in some parts of the world still is. The first powered loom was invented in 1830 in England. Looms have become faster and more efficient ever since, to the point of sophistication where they are continuous operations. Right now, giant looms are running 24/7, rotating at 1200 RPM, while you may be sleeping, turning out enormous amounts textiles at very low cost.

It's hard to appreciate the high speed and continuous nature of these looms until you see one in action. I have include a YouTube link which shows exactly this.

http://www.youtube.com/watch?v=V5e1YKkZFhc

YouTube Search Terms: Loom
View this video, and the complexity that is involved in the setup of this machine, it would be hard to make the case that it would be a good use of time and the machine to setup all of the of the spindles and produce a different product. This is a textbook example of continuous manufacturing processes, the efficiency of continual use is simply so high it trumps many other factors. These weaving machines rotate at roughly 1200 RPM and are computer controlled.

Continuous processes require continual supplies of raw materials. Any shortage of raw materials would mean stopping the process, which would result in significant inefficiencies. Continuous manufacturing processes have the highest efficiency, the lowest per unit cost, but also the highest investments in machinery. Continuous manufacturing is the eventual state when variability has been controlled in the manufacturing process and the process has been fully automated.

In case one might conclude that continuous manufacturing is simply for production efficiency and cost reduction, pharmaceuticals are an example of an industry that leverage long production runs for quality reasons.

> *"In this manufacturing model, specific quantities of a drug are produced to fill an order (batch) and quality is assessed through sampling, using destructive analytical tests and measurements. If the quality standards are not met, the entire batch is rejected and sent back for reprocessing. It is estimated that rejected batches, rework and investigations can use as much as 25% of pharmaceutical company revenues. Though batch processing is tried and true, it is inherently wasteful and often complicates future project planning because manufacturing design and scale-up for a new drug. In comparison, within a continuous manufacturing model, raw materials are put into an automated system that is capable of carrying out complex chemical tests according to predetermined quality parameters. These quality checks occur throughout the manufacturing process and without interruptions. Rejected products can be handled through recycling loops, enabling the reuse of some or all component parts."*
>
> – World Pharmaceuticals

If there is one industry that faces little price pressure in it's manufacturing, it is the patent (as opposed to the generic) pharmaceutical industry. However, they have stayed with long production runs primarily because it increases product quality.

Furthermore, continuous operations, as with repetitive (or simply longer or larger production runs applied to discrete or batch manufacturing)are also easier to model than shorter production run environments. Of course, what applies to any of the manufacturing categories, applies to the changes in production run length within that category. This is explained in the quotations below from PlanetTogether.

> *"In a multi-stage production, it's often the case that material flows out of one piece of equipment directly into another with no storage*

*in between. For example, a hot dog manufacturer may grind beef in the grinder while the ground beef is fed directly into a stuff line. If each grinder has a one-to-one fixed connection to one stuff line then the process can simply be modeled as a single operation. **However if each grinder makes products that can feed multiple varying stuff lines then this presents a scheduling challenge.** As material is made by one operation, it is creating intermediate material at a particular rate. This material is then consumed at a particular (perhaps varying) rate. In our example, a grinder may be making beef that is consumed by multiple stuff lines simultaneously(which perhaps start at different times and run at different rates). This is handled by PlanetTogether by automatically examining the cumulative production and consumption rates of the material over time and ensuring that the resulting schedule is feasible that enough beef is being ground to feed the pack lines as scheduled."*

– Using PlanetTogether for Effective Scheduling in the
Process Industry

Therefore the scheduling complexity must also be accounted for in any movement to shorter production runs. Shorter production runs result in more changeovers – the technical term used in production planning and scheduling to describe the activity of moving from producing one product to producing another product, or beginning a new production run. Changeover costs change in their magnitude depending upon the particular manufacturing situation. I have deliberately provided examples of manufacturing scenarios where changeover costs are very high; primarily to illustrate the fact that there are many manufacturing situations that simply can't be made flexible. However, changeover costs exit in every manufacturing situation. Even in a job shop, where items are individually made, the more the following item differs from the previous item, the higher the cost of production and longer the production process. These costs are of often modeled or attempted to be modeled in production planning and scheduling applications. Most applications of this type will use a table to store either the costs and or the duration that it requires to perform the changeover. These applications will sometimes have the capability to changeover the production schedule in a way that minimizes the costs and durations which can either be performed by the internal logic of the application (usually an optimizer) or by making the costs apparent to the production scheduler such that they manually move the production orders in sequence in such a way that the changeover costs or durations are reduced. The following is an example of such a changeover table.

Changeover Matrix/Table

From Product	To Product	Changeover Time (In Hours)	Changeover Cost (in Dollars)
White Paint	Yellow Paint	1.5	$ 550.00
Yellow Paint	White Paint	3.0	$ 1,100.00
White Paint	Dark Blue Paint	1.5	$ 550.00
Dark Blue Paint	White Paint	4.0	$ 1,466.67
Yellow Paint	Dark Blue Paint	2.0	$ 733.33
Dark Blue Paint	Yellow Paint	4.0	$ 1,466.67

The author of the earlier listed quotation who referred to *"challenging the "one size fits all" assumption of traditional mass production,"*and many from Sales and Marketing in addition to proponents of Lean Manufacturing, make it sound as if they are oppressed by manufacturing interests that force them into some type of "one size fits all" or "mass produced" approach which limits their flexibility. This is hardly the case; in my experience, manufacturing tends to be weaker politically than any of these other groups. What manufacturing communicates to these groups is that there are specific limitations to manufacturing, the limitations that have been explained in this chapter. These are simply the rules that manufacturing must follow. Certainly, one can choose to produce in smaller batches, but **not without** increases in costs, reductions in capacity and normally decreases in product quality.

"Savvy executives are beginning to realize that the millions of dollars invested in implementing sophisticated ERP systems have failed to provide any competitive advantage. They will soon come

to understand that ERP has its roots in mass production, an increasingly irrelevant business strategy and conflicts with twenty-first century customer needs and expectations. And these same executives will be looking closely at companies like Dell to find a more relevant and effective business strategy – a strategy called mass customization."

The first part of this quotation is true – and is the subject of the SCM Focus Press Book, *The Real Story behind ERP: Separating Fact from Fiction.* However, I disagree that executives realize this as ERP systems are as of this publishing still the largest category of enterprise software on the basis of sales revenues. Also, ERP is not particularly wedded to any manufacturing environment. Although it is true that ERP is not particularly good at planning any manufacturing environment. The vast majority of ERP systems provide mediocre or weak manufacturing capabilities. However, such systems are equally bad at manufacturing in any environment (from MTS to ETO). It also seems to be a projection to state that mass production is increasingly irrelevant. In fact, we continue to rely upon mass production for a very wide range of products that would be quite expensive if they were produced in smaller batches with frequent changeovers. Examples of this include lightbulbs, petroleum refining, mining, consumer electronics – in fact there are more examples of mass produced items than there are examples of customized items. Finally, in referencing Dell, it should be noted that Dell was able to maintain an ATO manufacturing environment because it sold its computers online and was selling a configurable product. Dell was very popular with companies, which tend to heavily configure their computers. However, while the author is probably right that many companies may look longingly towards Dell and the assemble to order manufacturing environment, as has been covered, not all or even that high of a percentage of manufacturers fit with this model. For instance, the executive who works for a pen company is not going to be able to move his or her company to an ATO manufacturing environment because there is little demand and little willingness to pay the premium for custom pens. Companies that have tried mass customization that were not good fits for it are explained in the following quotation:

"Industry leaders, including Toyota, Dow Jones, and Motorola, have

tried to employ mass customization but many have failed. Toyota, for example, understated the increase in complexity related to its intention of timely delivering a custom made car. Lately several large companies such as Levis and Apple, have implemented mass customization successfully. However the innovation space has remained small and the share of total revenue likewise. A couple of years ago I discussed this issue with Frank Piller, a leading researcher in Mass Customization who has worked with several big companies and their mass customization initiatives including Adidas. He claimed that about 80 percent of mass customization is about brand building and for consumer goods mass customization is utilized primarily to increase existing sales of mass produced products. During the last couple of years I have been stating that mass customization is a great for brand building, but it does not substantially drive revenue because it by nature is difficult to reach a high consumption volume through a 1:1 offering due to the impediments described above."

– Nike ID: The First Example of Mass Customization
Driving Revenue?

This brings up the topic of why mass customization is being done. Brand building means that it increases the prominence of the brand –there is a marketing benefit. And to the author's point above, it is difficult to reach a high consumption volume with mass customized products. Therefore, this is not a sustainable business model for a large percentage of the company's production (for most companies). Instead this is something done to increase the sales of mass produced items –much of the mass customization that is performed should probably be charged to Marketing.

Now let us return to the concerning quotations on the topic of mass customization.

"ERP offerings such as SAP and Oracle are optimized for mass production, not for mass customization; new technology that augments ERP is required to support mass customization."

I believe it is technically inaccurate to state that SAP or Oracle ERP systems are optimized for a mass production environment. Both SAP and Oracle have requirement strategies, with SAP's requirement strategies being explained in Chapter 3. SAP allows the user to flex between all of the manufacturing environments. These controls also adjust the forecast consumption, the main linchpin between demand planning and supply planning. This allows for this control to be customized per product location combination and therefore at multiple points within a BOM or recipe. As for the second part of the quote, new technology does exist that is far superior in manufacturing planning than anything inside of SAP or Oracle ERP systems – but these technologies add value to all of the manufacturing environments. It may possibly be true that these new software systems benefit some of the manufacturing environments over the others, I do not see why this would necessarily be the case. ERP systems are really primarily designed for managing transactions – creating purchase orders, stock transfer orders, accounting entries. They are not optimized for planning and never have been. Software designed to carry out that function will always have advantages, no matter the requirement strategy chosen.

Everything Old is New Again

Another issue with how mass customization is presented is that it is presented as something new. However, shorter production runs are not at all new. One of the primary reasons for the improvement in standards of living was the move from **short production runs to longer production runs**. This was enabled through the application of first on site coal generated power plants and later remote power plants that lead to the electrification of the production process. This is referred to as the **first and second industrial revolutions**.[3] Mass

---

[3] Fossil fuels and the growth of manufacturing that occurred during the fist and second industrial revolutions are often written about as separate phenomena, but in fact they reinforced one another. The first industrial revolution was powered with by the localized combustion of fossil fuels. This greatly increased the power that was available to manufacturing, and allowed manufacturing to be flexibly located, instead of having to locate manufacturing next to natural power sources, such as rivers. In Europe, mills, such as those designed for grinding grain, malt and meal were most often located next to rivers so that the waterpower could be harnessed to perform the grinding. However waterwheels -- where the shaft was connected to gears and a series of belts and pulleys, was also used in manufacturing. In the first industrial revolution, most factories either had their own on site steam engine, or a power building placed in the middle of small

production is what allowed for the costs of manufactured items to decline and to create broad based consumer markets in everything from appliance to automobiles – products that had previously only been available to the rich. Many individuals do not understand the enormous efficiencies of mass production and think in terms of having their cake and eating it too. They want the efficiencies of long production runs along with the flexibility, lower inventories and human element of short production runs. We rejected this possibility nearly a century ago and reaped the benefits.

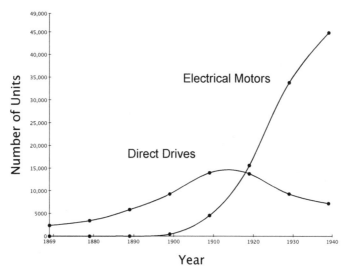

This shows how electrical drives (unit drives) took over for direct drives in factories. From roughly 1919 being completely inconsequential in factories, electric-powered unit drives surpass direct drives (line shaft driven) by 1920

This was enabled through the invention of electrification and the electrical grid. Electrification, or the development of the electrical grid occurred from the 1880s to 1950 in the US and the UK. On premises, steam engines drove manufacturing machinery in 1900. However, by 1920, remote electricity, at first by a remote steam engine and then later by a remote steam turbine , driving electrical motors on the factory floor, was more common in driving machinery

---

factories that could be rented, with a single steam engine powered a shaft for each rental factory that surrounded the power building.

than locally generated power. The growth of centralized power generation was very fast. By 1914 the power generated by electrical utilities surpassed all the power produced at factories in the US.

Notice the line above. The shaft here is connected to multiple pulleys (the cylinders) which transfer the power to another pulley below which was connected to what was called the driving spindle, which the drives the machine. A pulley not connected to the driving spindle was called the "idler" and was essentially neutral. The belt was put on the idler either when the operator needed to switch gears, or when the machine was not in use. Not consuming any of the power from the steam engine. However, the top pulley still needed to turn, and any turning pulley still consumed energy in the form of friction. It is estimated that the power loss across the shaft was normally more than 25%, and roughly 1/3 to 2/3s of the power created in the factory's steam engine was consumed in the friction of turning the various shafts. From their invention, many improvements were made in the belt (changed to rope) and to the pulley (The diameter of the pulleys were increased to improve mechanical efficiency.)

Henry Ford attributed the unit electrical drive, and the ability to locate it flexibly along an assembly line as instrumental to being able to configure the assembly lines in a way that maximized productivity.

Conclusion
So we have discussed each of the downsides to shorter production runs individually, but let's now review each of the downsides together.

1. Higher Costs

2. Lower Quality
3. Lower Productivity and Output
4. Infeasible for the Production of Many Products

As yet, proponents have not come up with novel ways to reduce these negatives, they simply propose that the benefits to short production runs are high.

Mass customization is primarily an aspirational concept which creates unrealistic expectations. It's sold as an idea using very weak evidence, and is most appealing to those that know the least about manufacturing. It is true that product proliferation is increasing, but the generalizations taken from this are badly misapplied and most of the examples provided by mass customization proponents come from areas outside of manufacturing, or are very simple manufacturing scenarios (i.e. the Planters example).

Online retailing has grown tremendously and looks to continue to replace much offline retail. This provides more opportunities for assemble to order. Media such as books and DVDs are a very good example of this. This book you are reading was made to order, because book manufacturing technology has evolved to the point where books can be made one at a time (due to automation) although at a higher cost than long production runs. Of course book manufacturing is also quite simple. But these are exceptions.

However, what is misleading, with respect to the statements made about mass customization, is that the proponents seem to imply that something similar in terms of technological changes has occurred on the manufacturing floor, which is untrue. The Internet and web based store fronts do not change the costs and time required for changeovers. They do not change other lead times that are within the system. And the distinction between customer facing technologies versus manufacturing technologies and manufacturing constraints should be understood. In fact, these types of errors, overgeneralizing the technological innovation in one area to other areas is quite common with those that write on mass customization. The following quotation is a good example of this.

"Today, near-customization is rapidly becoming the norm.
Electronic tablets and mobile devices, for instance, allow us to access

increasingly specialized applications. Similarly, YouTube has just invested $100 million to create dozens of television-like channels that will cater to audiences with narrowly defined interests.

Even Amazon has gradually transformed itself from an Internet hypermarket to something closer to a clearinghouse that matches customer requests with near-customized products. We are entering an era in which it will be commonplace to order a bespoke shirt that will then be made in the cheapest location in the world."

–Brace for the Mass Customization Revolution

Here again, the YouTube example has nothing at all to do with, and has not changed the constraints on, the manufacturing floor. Amazon has become a dominant online retailer, but again this has not altered manufacturing. On the final point made by the quotation, although the labor may be inexpensive, custom shirts are still expensive to make. The rise of the Internet or Amazon did not impact or change the rules or limitations of manufacturing facilities.

CHAPTER 7

Forecast Consumption

One of the areas of functionality that is, in part, controlled by the requirements strategy is **forecast consumption**. Forecast consumption is how the sales orders and the forecasts relate to one another in the supply planning system. The concept is that, further out on the planning horizon, the forecast drives the supply plan. The forecast can be considered a placeholder for the actual demand – which is the sales orders. As the sales orders arrive, in order to prevent double counting demand, the sales orders decrement from the forecast, or "consume" the forecast. The common controls for forecast consumption are the following:

1. *Requirements Strategy*: This controls if sales orders consume the forecast, of if the forecast is even used at all. For instance, finished goods that are MTO or ATO do not use the forecast in any way, even if a forecast is loaded into the supply planning system.

2. *Forward or Backward Consumption*: This setting controls how far forward and how far backward consumption of the forecast by sales orders occurs. Backward forecast consumption means that current sales orders can go backward as many days as

the system is configured in order to consume the forecast. Forward forecast consumption means the current sales orders can go forward as many days as the system is set in order to consume the forecast. The forecasts for prior periods are being applied to future periods, allowing the remainder of unconsumed forecast quantities to be consumed by periods of high sales orders.

3. *Consumption Mode*: Controls the direction on the time axis in which the system consumes the forecast (Options are: Backward consumption, Backward/forward consumption, Forward consumption).

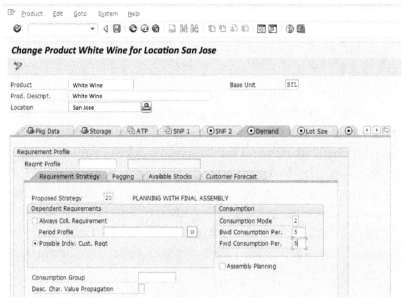

This is an example of the forecasting consumption settings in the application SAP SNP.

In order to understand how forecast consumption works in an application in detail, let's review different forecast consumption settings in a spreadsheet. This is how the values would display within the application, but the spreadsheet is easier to follow. Below is a spreadsheet mockup of the SAP Planning Book and its logic shown on the following page provides an example of where forecast consumption induces over-ordering. The SAP Planning Book is the main view into the planning system. The overall orders that would be generated are compared both with and without backward consumption. The key figures without backward consumption are highlighted in light pink.

		Initial (Past 5 Calendar Days)	Monday	Tuesday	Wednesday	Thursday	Friday	Totals
	Actual Forecast	*6,000*	*2,000*	*2,000*	*2,000*	*2,000*	*2,000*	*10,000*
Demand	Forecast (*unconsumed forecast*) - with 5 day backward consumption		-	-	-	-	500	*500*
	Forecast (*unconsumed forecast*) - with no backward consumption	1,000	500	500	-	-	500	*2,500*
	Sales Orders		1,500	1,500	5,000	3,200	1,500	*12,700*
	Production or procurement orders with backward consumption		1,500	1,500	5,000	3,200	2,000	*13,200*
	Production or procurement orders with no backward consumption		2,000	2,000	5,000	3,200	2,000	*14,200*

Here we can see that the sales order of 5,000 units consumes unconsumed forecast from the previous periods. This adjusts the production or procurement orders down for Monday and Tuesday and may have also reduced the production or procurement orders from the initial column, depending upon when the sales order was recorded in the system. Secondly, the total order quantity with five-day backward consumption is closer to the actual demand for that period.

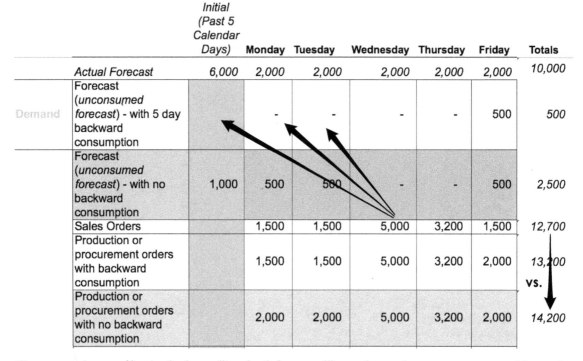

	Initial (Past 5 Calendar Days)	Monday	Tuesday	Wednesday	Thursday	Friday	Totals
Actual Forecast	6,000	2,000	2,000	2,000	2,000	2,000	10,000
Forecast (*unconsumed forecast*) - with 5 day backward consumption		-	-	-	-	500	500
Forecast (*unconsumed forecast*) - with no backward consumption	1,000	500	500	-	-	500	2,500
Sales Orders		1,500	1,500	5,000	3,200	1,500	12,700
Production or procurement orders with backward consumption		1,500	1,500	5,000	3,200	2,000	13,200 vs.
Production or procurement orders with no backward consumption		2,000	2,000	5,000	3,200	2,000	14,200

Forecasts have effectively been "pushed forward" to where they are consumed by sales orders. Using neither backward nor forward consumption promotes an upward bias in ordering. With backward consumption enabled, the total demand is closer to the actual demand. Without the ability to consume from other periods, the high sales orders on Wednesday will convert to production or procurement orders, but previous periods where the forecast was higher are not reduced.

One additional outcome of the backward consumption displayed above was to push the ordering forward to match sales orders, rather than to match the forecast.

While this outcome is not discussed often, it is beneficial. When forward forecast consumption is enabled, future ordering based purely on forecasts is reduced;however, only backward consumption postpones the orders generated to better align with sales orders.

Now that we have covered how forecast consumption works and its benefits, let's delve into some interesting questions regarding forecast consumption.

Implications to the Question of Backward Forecast Consumption

Here are some questions that should be discussed when explaining forecast consumption:

1. What is the purpose of forecast consumption in the same period? (In fact, one can set the forecast consumption to have zero forward and backward consumption, so that sales orders decrement the forecast only within the same period.)

2. What is the purpose of using backward or forward consumption? It is beneficial to observe (and also to describe to planners) that same-period consumption -- and consumption that is either backward or forward – accomplishes two different objectives:

   - *Same-period Forecast Consumption:* This is intended to prevent double counting when calculating the total demand that will then be used to drive production, procurement or stock transfers. Same-period Forecast Consumption is one method of having forecasts and sales orders interoperate in a way that allows forecasts to serve as a placeholder for sales orders(forecasts are then gradually replaced by sales orders as time passes).However, forecast consumption is only one way to do this. There are atleast two others, as I will explain in following section:

   - *Forecast Consumption Outside of the Same Period:* This is designed to prevent over-ordering. Over-ordering can occur when consumption is limited to the same periods by disallowing backward or forward consumption. While sales orders that are higher than forecasts are considered in the total demand calculation, sales orders that are lower than the forecast are not considered in total demand. Therefore, a forward or backward consumption setting (or both, as both backward and forward consumption can be configured in most supply planning systems) allows sales orders in one period to search and consume forecasts that have not yet been consumed in other periods. Products that are ordered more frequently tend to be given shorter backward/forward consumption durations, while products that are ordered less frequently tend to be given longer durations.

Alternatives to Forecast Consumption

There are several alternatives to forecast consumption that can achieve similar ends.

1. *Take the Greater of the Forecast or the Sales Orders:* One alternative method is to simply take the larger of the two values. In this way there is no forecast consumption; the forecast equals total demand until the sales orders exceed the forecast, at which point the sales orders equal total demand. The relationship between sales orders and forecast can change along the time horizon. For instance, some companies take the larger of the forecast or sales orders until five days out from the current date. At that point the forecasts are removed from the supply planning system, the logic being that only the sales orders should count when close to the execution horizon.

2. *Within a Certain Horizon Do Not Count the Forecast*: This method is actually another timing setting in APO called the SNP Forecast Horizon. That is the Horizon,in calendar days, during which the forecast is not considered as part of the total demand. Within this horizon, SNP does not take the forecast into account when calculating total demand. Outside of this horizon, the system calculates total demand using either the forecast or sales orders (which ever value is larger), and the other demands (dependent demand, distribution demand, planned demand, and confirmed demand). For instance, if the SNP Forecast Horizon is set to three weeks, then within this first three weeks of the SNP Planning Horizon, only sales orders count as demand.

CHAPTER 8

Variant Configuration in SAP ERP

Configurable products require special functionality in order to account for the complexity of configuration without greatly increasing the necessity to store very large amounts of master data in the ERP system in order to account for each configuration variant. Variant configuration is the name of the functionality in SAP ERP of developing a specific variant of a product based upon the combined selection of products. This greatly reduces the number of BOMs and routings and other associated master data that must be managed. Let us illustrate this with an example. Imagine if a finished good product has options in 10 different categories (color, trim level, etc..). If the 10 different categories have an average of 4 options, this would come out to 1,048,576 BOMs – which would not be feasible to keep as individual BOMs in a system. Unless one has worked with configurable products, it can be difficult to relate to environments where there are so many options. For instance, BMW has 2500 possible wiring harnesses, the different wiring harnesses are primarily driven by the specific options that are selected by the variant – with power required for some combination of components in some variants but not others. More examples of the available combinations in specific parts of a BMW include the following:

- 18 owner's manual languages
- 500 side-mirror combinations
- 1,300 front-bumper combinations
- 5,000 possible seat combinations
- 9,000 center-console combinations

One might ask if all of these options are really necessary and how they impact costs, however, that analysis is rarely performed. Operations are normally expected to simply manage the complexity and companies generally do not perform internal analysis projects that estimate the costs of having so many options.[1]The following quotation provides some background on the logic that supports configuration systems.

> *Configuration systems or also referred to as configurators or mass customization toolkits, are one of the most successfully applied Artificial Intelligence technologies. Examples are the automotive industry, the telecommunication industry,the computer industry and power electric transformers. Starting with rule-based approaches such as R1/XCON, model-based representations of knowledge (in contrast to rule-based representations) have been developed which strictly separate product domain knowledge from the problem solving one. There are two commonly cited conceptualizations of configuration knowledge. The most important concepts in these are components, ports, resources and functions. This separation of product domain knowledge and problem solving knowledge increased the effectiveness of configuration application development and maintenance since changes in the product domain knowledge do not affect search strategies and vice versa.*
>
> – Wikipedia

Configurable products are where there are many options to the product that can be selected. Examples of highly configurable products include automobiles

---

[1] This topic is delved into deeply in the SCM Focus Press book Promotions Forecasting: Forecast Adjustment Techniques in Software

and industrial machinery, but there are many others. Within a system, variant configuration applies both on the sales side and on the production side. Sales configurators are all over the Internet, with the Honda website being one example of this.

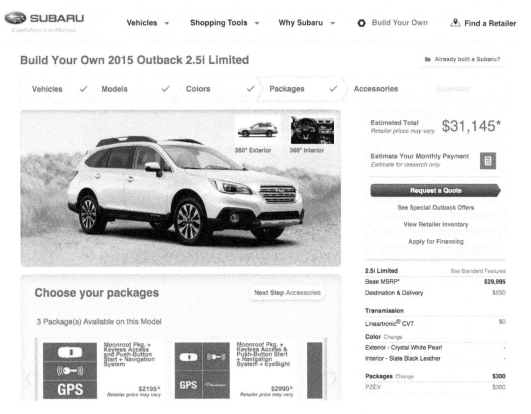

All of the automotive manufacturers now have online configurators, which allow the potential customer to choose their own configuration. Here I am configuring a Subaru and choosing the moonroof package, GPS and a number of options.

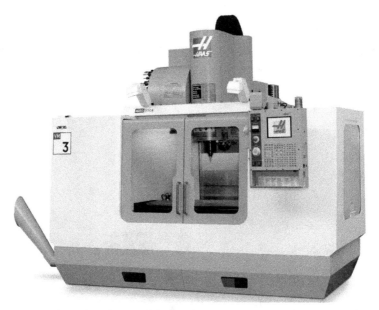

Haas Automation makes CNC machines that automate the manufacturing of parts. Haas Automation uses variant configuration functionality in order to manage the complexity of having highly configurable products.

Variant configuration is a functionality that interacts with a number of pre-existing functionalities within the SAP ERP system. These include the following areas:

- CA *Classification*
- *LO Material Master*
- *PP Bill of Material*
- *PP Routings*
- *PP–PI Master Recipes*
- *SD Sales*
- *SD Conditions*
- *MM Purchasing*
- *CO Costing*
- *PP Material Requirements Planning (MRP)*
- *PP Production Orders - SAP*

As an example of the major interconnections of variant configuration, if one variant over another is sold, it has direct implications to cost. When a particular variant is produced, it also has cost implications. Variant configuration allows any choice in any characteristic to be applied to the cost of the finished good. This way each variant that is produced has a specific cost that may be different from the cost of any other variant that is produced.

Some configuration products are produced in a build to order manufacturing environment, but they don't need to be. Many companies that use variant configuration in a BTS or ATO environment, therefore the sales order can either **precede** or **follow** the production order.

When a particular variant is planned for production, it leads to the procurement of different input items. If the sales orders are placed before the production orders, then the procurement is also based upon the sales order. If the sales orders are placed after the production orders, then the procurement is based upon a forecast. For companies that have configurable products, being either a MTO or ATO manufacturing environment is highly desirable. One might presuppose that following a MTS manufacturing strategy is very difficult to apply for configurable products; however, often companies do have a good idea of what the popular configurations are that will be demanded. Furthermore, companies have the ability to perform demand shaping. That is, the company can move demand from one variant to another by either pushing it through education/marketing, or providing discounts and other incentives to their customers. A perfect example of this is the automotive industry where customers have the option of purchasing a car that is a very close, but often not perfect match for their desired configuration that is either available on the lot, or can be transferred from another lot, or may choose to wait, and switch to placing a special order. This does not stop Ford, which has configurable products, from employing make to stock; and, in fact, few customers actually choose to wait and place a special order. In fact, most automotive plants are designed for a MTS manufacturing environment with special orders tending to have often strangely lengthy lead times.

As is normally the case, MTO customers tend to buy more options and tend to be higher profit customers. This has been recognized by companies so much that BMW has developed a marketing program to switch customers from MTS to MTO vehicles. This is explained in the following quotation.

> *Vehicle customization on a mass scale has been the Holy Grail of the auto industry for more than a decade, with little success. Americans are an impatient lot. They've been trained to sacrifice a few features or accept a different color if they can get a great deal on a car they can drive home immediately.*

> *James O'Donnell, BMW's most senior U.S. executive, wants to change that and, in the process, maybe change the way cars are made in America. BMW is launching a marketing push to convince more American consumers to order their car exactly the way they want it and take delivery in two to six weeks. To entice them, BMW will offer them unique choices and provide a video link of their car being "born" while they're waiting for delivery. The push coincides with a $750 million expansion at the Spartanburg plant to make room for a second SUV, the redesigned X3.- Forbes*

With variant configuration functionality, instead of creating a different BOM for every finished good sold, which would be a problem when there are many options and therefore many variants, variant configuration allows for an all-inclusive BOM to be created. Then, for specific components, they can be included or excluded in the sales BOM. Creating a configurable material in SAP, a so-called "super BOM", enables this process.

This is explained in the book *Variant Configuration with SAP*, and the following is a quote from that book:

> *Another elementary part of Variant Configuration is the variant bill of materials (BOM). The BOM of a configurable material enables the automatic deactivation of BOM items. If a selection condition is linked to an item, then the item only becomes effective if the selection condition is linked to an item, then the item only becomes effective if the selection condition is met. Similarly, you can deactivate entries of the variant routing via selection conditions. You can calculate certain*

fields, such as the BOM item quantity or items for the operation. For
this purpose, you assign procedures to a BOM item or an entry into
the routing.

In addition to a super BOM, variant configuration has a super routing, or all
of the operations that apply the super BOM. Some combination of routings are
used for some variants but are not used for other variants. All possible routing
permutations are included in the super routing. Variant configuration increases the complexity of any implementation, but decreases the maintenance effort
that would otherwise be required to manage individual BOMs and routings for
configurable products.

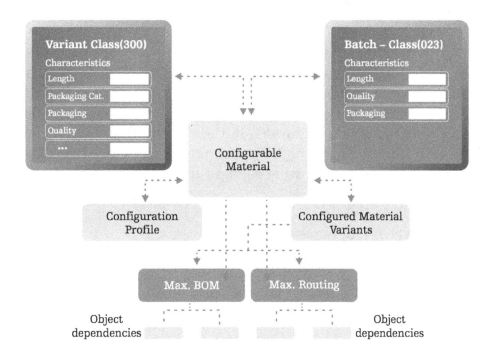

In this graphic, but ITC InfoTech, the super BOM and super routing are referred to as
"max" BOM and routing.

Variant configuration allows for two tasks to be assigned: high level configuration (where production options are selected) and lower level configuration

(where the BOM is exploded and the routings are applied. Variant configuration in SAP answers the following questions:

- Whether the required variant can be produced
- What price you can quote for the product.
- Whether the customer's specifications can be covered from stock.[2]

The Super BOM and the Super Routing

The super BOM also interacts with a super routing. If one imagines comparing two variants that are identical to one another except for the option of installing a module within the product, the variant without one of the modules means the routing changes. One finished good variant is sent to the workstation to install the module, and the other variant skips this step.

Setting up Variant Configuration

The first step to using variant configuration is to establish the material as a configurable product. A company can choose to setup whatever percentage of their overall product database as configurable or standard/non-configurable.[3]Materials must be defined as configurable in the system. Once a material has been defined as a configurable product, it must have a configurable profile. The configuration profile has the following configuration settings:

- Is the material for Planned Production Orders?
- Is the material for Sales Orders?
- Does the material apply for Order BOMs?
- Should the BOM explosion be performed, and if so should it be a multi-level BOM?
- Define the application for the BOM explosion (normally PP-Production Planning)

---

[2] *http://www.slideshare.net/eddai/variant-configurationforbeginnersbeginnersguide*

[3] Materials aren't the only objects that can be set as configurable,

- The Level of Detail of the to be applied, restricted to only Configurable Assemblies.

The material can be setup with the following alternatives:

- For what configurable plant does the material apply?

- What is the effectively date of the configurable material?

- Is the configurable material Sales and Distribution or just for Engineering?[4]

- Whether the configurable result should apply to the BOM or instead to a Task List.

Now that we have established the material and how it will used. We need to setup the specific configuration of the alternatives. Within variant configuration, the characteristics are setup, which then allows for a selection of options. This is done with Characteristic Value Assignment. So for a computer the following characteristics might be setup.

- Type

- CPU

- RAM

- Graphics Card

- Computer Case

Once the characteristics are setup, then the options per characteristics are setup. This combination of individual characteristics then encompasses the universe of variants that the company offers.

---

[4] Actually, the SCM Focus Press book *The Bill of Materials in Excel, Planning, ERP and PLM/BMMS Software* calls into question whether BOMs should ever be created as design BOMs in ERP systems. ERP vendors have tended to oversell the capabilities of their systems to act as fully functional BOM management systems. BOM management systems offer many advantages over using ERP systems to control the BOM. One important feature which explains why is that engineering and design do not tend to use the ERP system.

Setting Up the Configurable BOM or Recipe

After the material has been fully setup as a configurable material with its characteristics, it is necessary to setup a different type of BOM that then interacts with this finished goods material. A configurable BOM is called a super BOM. A super BOM is the following:

The bill of material (BOM) of a configurable material contains all the components that are required to manufacture the material. The BOM contains components that are only used in specific variants (variant parts), as well as components that are used in all variants (non-variable parts).– SAP

Therefore, in the example that was provided above, if a finished good has 10 categories where there are 4 options per category or characteristic, then each option must be defined as an option within the super BOM.

Setting Up the Configurable Routing

The routing is the connection between the BOM and the work centers in the factory. A configurable routing simply declares the relationship between the different finished goods variants in a flexible way that allows the routing or super routing to adjust to the super BOMs the super BOM can be planned and produced. Setting up each routing options within the routing performs this activity. In the same way as the super BOM, the super routing automatically adjusts the routing to the particular BOM variant that is selected. Variant configuration functionality outputs the routing based upon the final variant that is selected. This allows planning to be performed, so that the load on the resources adjusts depending upon the variant ultimately selected.

Conclusion

Configurable products insert very significant complexity into an ERP system and associated systems such as BOM management systems and external planning systems. Variant configuration is how configurable products can be efficiently managed in the SAP ERP system. The purpose of this chapter has been to simply provide a taste for how one ERP system manages variants. For a detailed explanation of variant configuration, see the book *Variant Configuration with SAP*. The majority of companies that make configurable products use some variant configuration capability within their systems, and when this happens, the functionality that controls variants must interact with many different areas of functionality. Variant configuration is used in all of the different manufacturing environments.

Conclusion

Manufacturing environments are important to the setup of supply chain planning and execution systems. An important feature of the various manufacturing environments is that the relationship between the demand signal and the beginning of production or procurement is not always the same for all of the products in the BOM or recipe. This is referred to as the **replenishment trigger**. The production order can precede or follow the sales order, and materials can be input items inventories by the company before a sales order in the case of make to stock and assembled order or input items can be procured after the sales order is received in the case of make to order. Replenishment triggers are actions that cause replenishment to occur. The term **replenishment** is easy to comingle in one's mind with **purchasing**. However, the replenishment strategy drives both procured materials and produced materials. To replenish simply means to fill again. Within a supply network, which is an association of locations – factories, distribution centers, retail locations, etc. has a series of stocking location. Supply planning is the determination of the timing and quantity of replenishment across this supply network.

It is sometimes proposed by executives within companies that they can switch their manufacturing environment. However, an important feature of the various manufacturing environments is that the relationship between the demand signal and the beginning of production or procurement is not always the same for all of the products in the BOM or recipe. For instance, in Make-to-Stock, all procurement and production is performed before the sales order is received. In both Engineering-to-Order and Make-to-Order all of the procurement and production is performed after a sales order is received – with the products in the BOM for Engineering-to-Order being procured and produced the latest after the sales order is received as, at the time of the receipt of the sales order, it is not known exactly what is to be built. While it is sometimes presented this way, the manufacturing environments that are available to a company have less to do with what the company "wants to do," and more to do with the particular product the companies produces combined with the type of market that the product is sold to.

How the forecasts **and orders** are managed or used by the supply planning system is normally referred to as the requirements strategy. One of the complexities of the requirements strategy is that it is assigned within the supply planning system **at each** product location combination. However, when one speaks of a requirements strategy it is easy to lapse into the oversimplified view that a BOM has a single requirements strategy, when in fact, a BOM really has a combination of **requirements strategies**.

Forecast consumption is how the sales orders and the forecasts relate to one another in the supply planning system. The concept is that further out on the planning horizon the forecast drives the supply plan. The forecast can be considered a placeholder for the actual demand – which is the sales orders. As the sales orders arrive, in order to prevent double counting demand the sales orders decrement from the forecast, or "consume" the forecast.

There is a great deal of conversation or hype around what is called mass customization. However, adding options and configurability to manufacturing increases the complexity on the manufacturing floor. Making more customized items means shorter manufacturing lead times and means more changeover costs, and lower production efficiency (more time in setups means less time for production time) and also has negative quality implications as when a new production run is initiated, it will often mean more waste as the tuning process can be required when at the beginning of the production run. The further away one is from manufacturing and the less time one spends visiting real factories or working in them, the more feasible no cost or low cost flexible manufacturing/mass customization appears. The evidence provided to support mass customization as a viable manufacturing strategy is extraordinarily weak. And the examples provided often do not come from manufacturing, are very simple manufacturing changes or explain a change that was made without any of the supporting numbers to show what the change cost, what the gains were from the change, etc.. Examples In fact some of the well-known mass customization case studies are justified on the basis of **marketing benefits rather than on profitability.** Something which is greatly misunderstood is that mass production is where the efficiencies in manufacturing are primarily obtained. Light bulbs are not custom designed, and they do not need to be. The fact that light bulbs are standardized and produced on repetitive manufacturing production lines is what allows light bulbs to be affordable to anyone. Mass production a primary basis of the standard of living in the developed countries, and customized manufacturing, which was the primary manufacturing mode prior to mass production resulted in often large variances and high prices that restricted mass consumption. There will always be a place for customized manufacturing – bespoke suits are a great example of this, but this is not the great bulk of manufacturing activity that takes place due to factors ranging from lead times to productivity limitations.

This misunderstanding of manufacturing history and how manufacturing actually works comes from a lack of real experience with and exposure to real manufacturing environments.[1]

---

[1] One of the most common approaches is for software vendors to develop a discrete solution, and then simply sell it into the other manufacturing environments for which it is a poor match by proposing to executive decision makers that their discrete solution can meet all of their needs. This can and does go on for years. I have seen applications that were never designed to meet the requirements of the process industry be continually sold into process industry accounts with the previous failures of the application in similar clients never seeming to affect the ability to sell that product into new process industry clients. This is particularly true of companies that have a major brand.

Configurable products insert very significantly complexity into an ERP system and associated systems such as BOM management systems, external planning systems. Variant configuration is how configurable products can be efficiently or relatively managed in an ERP system. Variant configuration is used in all of the different manufacturing environments. However, this is a significant product complexity that results in reduced manufacturing productivity and higher prices. In some scenarios and with some products, this is absolutely necessary, and therefore the higher costs are accepted as the price of doing business.

Understanding the system implications to the various manufacturing environments is important to making better decisions in system selection and configuration. Supply planning and production planning applications contain the functionality to be configured to meet the different manufacturing environments, with some applications better at some environments over others. The starting point is always the proper interpretation of the business requirements.

References

Slate, America's Food Factories, Matthew Iglesias, September 14, 2012.
http://www.slate.com/articles/business/moneybox/2012/09/mcdonald_s_chipotle_star-bucks_fast_food_and_chain_restaurants_are_manufacturers_.html

Byrnes, Jonathan. Islands of Profit in a Sea of Red Ink. Portfolio Hardcover. 2010.

What Makes Engineer to Order (ETO) Products Unique? Arena Solutions.
http://www.arenasolutions.com/resources/articles/engineered-to-order

Variant Configuration, SAP
http://sapdocs.info/sap/sd-related-topics/variant-configuration/

http://help.sap.com/saphelp_46c/helpdata/en/d8/fa9bd49ede11d1903b0000e8a49aad/frameset.htm

http://www.forbes.com/forbes/2010/0927/companies-bmw-general-motors-cars-be-spoke-auto.html

http://sapdocs.info/sap/sd-related-topics/variant-configuration/

Parker, Akweil. How Long to Build a Ferrari. About. July 2010.
http://auto.howstuffworks.com/how-long-to-build-ferrari.htm

Flynn, Anthony. Flynn, Emily Vencat. Custom Nation: Why Customization Is the Future of Business and How to Profit From It. BenBella Books. 2012.

http://help.sap.com/saphelp_erp60_sp/helpdata/en/92/58c0fb417011d189e-c0000e81ddfac/content.htm

https://www.ted.com/talks/joseph_pine_on_what_consumers_want?lan-guage=en#t-120730

In the New Economics: Fast Food Factories? David Cay Johnson. New York Times, Feburary 20, 2004.

KANBAN Replenishment. SAP Help.
http://help.sap.com/saphelp_470/helpdata/en/95/e81fa4f57011d194aa0000e83dcfd4/content.htm

Pine, Joseph B. Mass Customization: The New Frontier in Business Competition, Harvard Business Review Press, October 1, 1992.

Srinivasan, Shuba, KoenPauwels, Dominique Hanssens, and MarnikDekimpe. Who Benefits from Price Promotions. Harvard Business Review. September 2002.

Sanyal, Sanjeev. Brace for the Mass Customization Revolution. The Japan Times. March 18, 2012.
http://www.japantimes.co.jp/opinion/2012/03/28/commentary/world-commentary/brace-for-the-mass-customization-revolution/#.U6CXaK1dWko

Shaun Snapp, *Promotions Forecasting: Forecasting Adjustments Techniques in Software,* SCM Focus Press, 2014.

Shaun Snapp, *Process Industry Manufacturing Planning: Business and Software Approaches for Process Industries,* SCM Focus Press, 2013.

Shaun Snapp, *Superplant: Creating a Nimble Manufacturing Enterprise with Adaptive Planning Software,* SCM Focus Press, 2013.

Shaun Snapp, *Supply Planning with MRP, DRP and APS Software,* SCM Focus Press, 2012.

Decker, David. Nike ID: The First Example of Mass Customization Driving Revenue. Crossroad Innovation. September 10, 2010.

Gardner, David J. Piller, Frank. Mass Customization: How to Build to Order, Assemble to Order, Configure to Order, Make to Order, and Engineer to Order Manufacturers Increase. 2009.

Byrnes, Jonathan. Islands of Profit in a Sea of Red Ink. Portfolio Hardcover. 2010.

Is Your Stuff Falling Apart? Stacy Mitchell, Grist, November 2011.
http://grist.org/business-technology/2011-11-11-is-your-stuff-falling-apart-thank-walmart/

Weber, Austin. The Build to Order Challenge.Assembly Magazine. March 21 2006.
http://www.assemblymag.com/articles/84357-the-build-to-order-challenge

Blumohr, Uwe. Munch, Manfred. Ukalovic, Marin. Variant Configuration with SAP. Galileo Press. 2010

http://www.slideshare.net/eddai/variant-configurationforbeginnersbeginnersguide

http://www.itcinfotech.com/Uploads/Events/PDF/SapForMillProducts.pdf

Wikipedia, February 16 2015
https://en.wikipedia.org/wiki/Knowledge-based_configuration

http://scn.sap.com/docs/DOC-25224

Duplex, Wikipedia, July 27 2013

http://en.wikipedia.org/wiki/Duplex_(telecommunications)

http://www.americanprecision.org/2011-12-09-21-27-05

http://en.wikipedia.org/wiki/Master_production_schedule

http://en.wikipedia.org/wiki/Perpetual_inventory
1960s: Isolated Systems

Manufacturing, Wikipedia, July 12 2013

https://en.wikipedia.org/wiki/Manufacturing

Vendor Acknowledgments and Profiles

I have listed brief profiles of each vendor with screen shots included in this book below.

Profiles:

SAP

SAP does not need much of an introduction. They are the largest vendor of enterprise software applications for supply chain management. SAP has multiple products that are showcased in this book, including SAP ERP and SAP APO.

www.sap.com

Demand Works

Demand Works is a best-of-breed demand-and-supply-planning vendor that emphasizes flexible and easy-to-configure solutions. This book only focuses on the supply planning functionality within their Smoothie product, which includes MRP and DRP.

http://www.demandworks.com

Author Profile

Shaun Snapp is the founder and editor of SCM Focus. SCM Focus is one of the largest independent supply chain software analysis and educational sites on the Internet.

After working at several of the largest consulting companies and at i2 Technologies, he became an independent consultant and later started SCM Focus. He maintains a strong interest in comparative software design, and works both in SAP APO as well as with a variety of best-of-breed supply chain planning vendors. His ongoing relationships with these vendors keep him on the cutting edge of emerging technology.

Primary Sources of Information and Writing Topics

Shaun writes about topics with which he has firsthand experience. These topics range from recovering problematic implementations, to system configuration, to socializing complex software and supply chain concepts in the areas of demand planning, supply planning and production planning.

More broadly, he writes on topics supportive of these applications, which include master data parameter management, integration, analytics, simulation and bill of material management systems. He covers management aspects of enterprise software ranging from software policy to handling consulting partners on SAP projects.

Shaun writes from an implementer's perspective and as a result he focuses on how software is actually used in practice rather than its hypothetical or "pure release note capabilities." Unlike many authors in enterprise software who keep their distance from discussing the realities of software implementation, he writes both on the problems as well as the successes of his software use. This gives him a distinctive voice in the field.

Secondary Sources of Information

In addition to project experience, Shaun's interest in academic literature is a secondary source of information for his books and articles. Intrigued with the historical perspective of supply chain software, much of his writing is influenced by his readings and research into how different categories of supply chain software developed, evolved, and finally became broadly used over time.

Covering the Latest Software Developments

Shaun is focused on supply chain software selections and implementation improvement through writing and consulting, bringing companies some of the newest technologies and methods. Some of the software developments that Shaun showcases at SCM Focus and in books at SCM Focus Press have yet to reach widespread adoption.

Education

Shaun has an undergraduate degree in business from the University of Hawaii, a Master of Science in Maritime Management from the Maine Maritime Academy and a Master of Science in Business Logistics from Penn State University. He has taught both logistics and SAP software.

Software Certifications

Shaun has been trained and/or certified in products from i2 Technologies, Servigistics, ToolsGroup and SAP (SD, DP, SNP, SPP, EWM).

Contact

Shaun can be contacted at: shaunsnapp@scmfocus.com

Abbreviations

ATO – Assemble to Order
BOM – Bill of Materials
BTO – Build to Order
ERP – Enterprise Resource Planning
MTO – Make to Order
MTS – Make to Stock

Links Listed in the Book by Chapter

Chapter 1:

http://www.scmfocus.com

http://www.scmfocus.com/supplyplanning

http://www.scmfocus.com/writing-rules/

http://www.scmfocus.com/scmfocuspress/supply-books/the-supply-planning-with-mrpdrp-and-aps-software-book/

http://www.scmfocus.com/scmfocuspress/supply-books/requirements-strategies/

Chapter 3:

http://www.scmfocus.com/supplyplanning/2014/04/10/mrp-requirements-calculator/

http://www.scmfocus.com/scmhistory/2012/08/the-history-of-mrp-and-drp/

http://www.scmfocus.com/productionplanningandscheduling/2013/04/22/multi-plant-superplant-planning-definition/

Chapter 4:

http://www.arenasolutions.com/resources/articles/engineered-to-order

http://www.scmfocus.com/demandplanning/2010/09/why-companies-are-selecting-the-wrong-supply-chain-demand-planning-systems/

http://www.youtube.com/watch?v=V5e1YKkZFhc

Chapter 5:

http://www.youtube.com/watch?v=V5e1YKkZFhc

Chapter 8:

http://www.slideshare.net/eddai/variant-configurationforbeginnersbeginnersguide

www.ingramcontent.com/pod-product-compliance
Lightning Source LLC
LaVergne TN
LVHW080100070326
832902LV00014B/2337